## ADVANCE PRAISE FOR *YOURS TRULY*

"Upbeat, practical, and immensely useful... Hagerty shares a simple, good-natured approach that can work for anyone. He shows you how to make sense of your life narrative, how to tell it engagingly— and how to have a surprisingly good time as you create the story you've always wanted to share."

—GEORGE ANDERS, Pulitzer Prize winner and author of
*The Rare Find and You Can Do Anything*

"James R. Hagerty, a specialist in lives well lived, has written a book to die for."

—DAVID SHRIBMAN, Pulitzer Prize winner and author of
*I Remember My Teacher*

"Nobody knows more than James R. Hagerty about the stories we tell of the recently departed—and how to make sure you leave behind a good one."

—CHARLIE JANE ANDERS, author of *All the Birds in the Sky*
and *Never Say You Can't Survive*

"James R. Hagerty's advice is spot on in his inimitable witty style."

—KAY POWELL, retired news obituary editor of the
*Atlanta Journal-Constitution*

"Hagerty's premise of writing our own obituary not only eliminates the possibility that someone will get our story wrong but also provides us with a guide for living here and now. The idea: write down how you want to be remembered and then live into it. This book sparkles with compelling stories—humorous, poignant, and engrossing. I couldn't put it down until I'd finished the very last sentence. It really is that good."

—MORT CRIM, author of *Anchored: A Journalist's Search for Truth*

"Acclaimed obituary writer James R. Hagerty provides practical tips, writing advice, and heartwarming stories for inspiration. He makes the case, in this highly readable and entertaining book, that every life story is worth telling!"

—S.J. PEDDIE, author of *Sonny: The Last of the Old Time Mafia Bosses*

"With gentle wit, deep empathy, and a reporter's sharp eye for detail, James R. Hagerty takes readers by the hand and guides them through the greatest story of all: their lives. This beautiful book will show you how to write your own obituary, but it will also show you a few things about how to live."

—BRYAN GRULEY, author of the award-winning *Starvation Lake mysteries*

"Like any good obituary, *Yours Truly* is meticulously crafted. James R. Hagerty leads the reader on a curious and unexpected journey on how to thoroughly document your life story. Only you can tease out the rich nuances of your life and get it down on paper. With years of experience as the obituary writer for the *Wall Street Journal*, he will guide and help you take control of your life story—your legacy."

—TODD HARRA, coauthor of
*Mortuary Confidential: Undertakers Spill the Dirt,*
*Over Our Dead Bodies: Undertakers Lift the Lid*, and
author of *Last Rites: The Evolution of the American Funeral*

# YOURS TRULY

# YOURS TRULY

*An Obituary Writer's Guide
to Telling Your Story*

## JAMES R. HAGERTY

CITADEL PRESS
Kensington Publishing Corp.
www.kensingtonbooks.com

CITADEL PRESS BOOKS are published by

Kensington Publishing Corp.
119 West 40th Street
New York, NY 10018

All Kensington titles, imprints, and distributed lines are available at special quantity discounts for bulk purchases for sales promotions, premiums, fund-raising, educational, or institutional use. Special book excerpts or customized printings can also be created to fit specific needs. For details, write or phone the office of the Kensington sales manager: Kensington Publishing Corp., 119 West 40th Street, New York, NY 10018, attn: Sales Department; phone 1-800-221-2647.

CITADEL PRESS and the Citadel logo are Reg. U.S. Pat. & TM Off.

ISBN: 978-0-8065-4207-2

First Citadel hardcover printing: January 2023

10 9 8 7 6 5 4 3 2 1

Printed in the United States of America

Library of Congress Control Number: 2022943478

First electronic edition: January 2023

ISBN: 978-0-8065-4208-9 (e-book)

*Dedicated to the memory of my sister
Carol Kay Hagerty Werner (1954–2011),
who had many stories to tell and not
enough time to tell them all*

*Death steals everything except our stories.*

—JIM HARRISON

# Contents

# *Introduction*

SOMEDAY THE STORY OF YOUR life will be written.

The only question is how well or badly it will be written—what sort of picture it will leave behind for friends and family members, including those not yet born.

This book is for anyone who wants their story to be fair, accurate, interesting, and maybe even inspiring. It explains how to make sure your story is told the way you want—and how thinking about and preparing that story can help you live a better life.

If you do nothing and leave things to chance, there are two possible ways your life story will be recorded here on earth.

First possibility: If you are famous—a movie star, a major-league athlete, a big-name politician, the CEO of a Fortune 100 company, or the inventor of, say, the air fryer—professional news reporters are likely to write brief summaries of your life. That doesn't let you entirely off the hook, though. They will be able to write a truer-to-life story if you have written or spoken in depth about your life, because, after all, you know the story far better than anyone else.

Second possibility: If you are like me and more than 99 percent of all other people, your story is likely to be written in haste by a friend or family member distracted by grief and the many urgent tasks of dealing with a death. And, I'm sorry to inform you, this well-meaning person will probably describe someone you wouldn't recognize. He or she will remember imperfectly, and perhaps only vaguely, all the interesting things you confided over the years. The story most likely will be solemn and dull, giving no hint of who you really were, what you were trying to do with your life, what you learned, and what you accomplished.

Someone will pay a fee to have this notice appear in small print in a newspaper and then linger indefinitely on a website such as Legacy.com as the official and totally inadequate record of your life.

I want something better for my life story—and for yours. That is why I am going to tell you how to write your own story, or at least to leave some notes or recordings to guide anyone who has to finish the job after you die.

No, telling your story is not another irksome task, like making a will or clearing out the attic. Telling your story is less difficult than you may imagine. Telling your story can be amusing. It can pay off in unexpected ways.

At a minimum, reading this book will show you how to ensure that the brief summary of your life that appears in print and online will be the sort of report card you want. But let's aim higher: I will also show you how to write a longer version of your story, akin to a short memoir or autobiography, for your friends and family—and also for you, while you're still living, even if you're still young, especially if you're still young. Telling the story of your life so far can serve as a checkup, helping you determine whether you are on course to achieving something worth remembering.

The same storytelling techniques apply to the shorter and longer versions of the tale you will leave behind.

I will urge you to ask yourself the same three questions I ask before writing the story of anyone's life in the *Wall Street Journal*:

> What were you trying to do with your life?
> Why?
> And how did it work out?

These are questions we should all ask ourselves from time to time, without waiting until we are on our deathbeds and it is too late to improve the script.

THIS BOOK INCLUDES numerous summaries of life stories as a way of showing how to write them and, perhaps more important, what you can learn from them. In my case, writing obituaries has reinforced a belief that successful people tend to be optimists—not in the sense of deluding themselves into believing that all is for the best in this world, but in the sense of feeling confident that they can find ways to cope and thrive in almost any situation, and that the world will somehow go on, at least in their lifetimes, despite evidence to the contrary. The link between optimism and success is not surprising but is important to remember.

Those who feel helpless and are certain that humanity is on the brink of extinction will always find less incentive to get out of bed and make an effort. As I write this book, the news of the world is not encouraging. Here's a coping strategy: After reading about the latest horrors on the front page, cheer yourself up by turning to the death columns. Obituaries remind us that, even in the darkest times, people with a strong dose of optimism, tempered by a realistic assessment of human nature and their own abilities, have found ways to flourish, recover from calamities, earn a living, fall in love, and discover the joys of sharing any windfall that comes their way.

AT SOME POINT in their lives, many people resolve to write down their memories. Most never get around to it. Summing up a lifetime sounds like a chore, forever less urgent than other things, but I will show you how to do it in a way that requires only a moderate investment of time and no gift for literary writing.

Drawing on examples from real-life stories, I'll explain and demonstrate what to put in, what to leave out, and what makes for a good story that people will want to read. By the end of this book, I think you'll agree with me that writing your life story is not painful, not morbid, and not a sign of vanity. Instead, it is an exercise that will enrich your life and the lives of those who read and learn from it.

At the *Wall Street Journal*, I'm famous for writing obituaries about people who weren't famous. Most of the obituaries I write are about people who were interesting and notable in some way but whose names were unknown to nearly all of us. "I'd never heard of that person," readers often tell me, "but the story was fascinating."

Though you may not realize it yet, your life story is interesting too, maybe even fascinating. Telling it may be the best gift you ever give to your friends, your family, and yourself.

PART ONE

*How and Why*

CHAPTER 1

# *My Inspiration: From* Worm Killers *to the* Wall Street Journal

As the only full-time obituary writer for the *Wall Street Journal*, I've written more than 800 life stories about little-known people as well as the famous, the should-have-been famous, the infamous, and the otherwise notable.

A few years ago, I embarked on a trickier task: writing my own obituary—or, as I think of it, my own life story.

The first question I faced was: Where to begin? I figured: Why not start at the beginning?

> My mother gave birth to me around noon on a cool and rainy summer day, July 30, 1956, in Minneapolis. Then she smoked a cigarette.

This intro will not strike everyone as a proper opening for an obituary. That's okay. One advantage of writing your own obituary is that you can do it your way. You can make it three paragraphs long or longer than this book. You can be chatty and gossipy or mysteriously discreet.

Don't think of "obituary" as that dull, formulaic thing you've seen in dreary death notices. Think of it as your life story, the one shot you have at preserving it. Remember the simple equation: obituary = life story.

In writing my own, I don't need to worry about what editors might think. I'm not writing for editors. I'm writing for myself and those few friends and family members who may one day care to know more about my life.

By writing my own obituary, I am practicing what I preach: Write your own story while you can. Don't leave it to family members, who are almost certain to make a hash of it.

> Write your own story while you can. Don't leave it to family members, who are almost certain to make a hash of it.

One thing I've known from the start: I don't want to follow the standard form for obituaries—a list of names, dates, and achievements, interspersed with flowery quotes exaggerating my nobility, generosity, and devotion to family. There will be no speculation about whether I have gone on to a better place. I will not write that I "passed away surrounded by family" because that might give readers the idea that my family feared I was about to leap off my deathbed and make a break for the door.

Instead, in plain and simple terms, I will attempt to explain what I was trying to do with my life and how things panned out.

Come to think of it, those questions are worth asking yourself in any case. If, say, once a week, or once a month, we asked ourselves a few questions—What am I aiming for? Why? Am I on target?—perhaps we would make better choices. We would know ourselves better. If we struggle to think of even one positive thing that might go into our obituary, it's time to reassess our game plan, or fire the coach.

Is it presumptuous to write your own obituary? Isn't that someone else's job? I don't think so.

No one else can do it better. Surely I am the only person who remembers that my journalism career began at age five, when I founded a short-lived, handwritten newspaper called *Worm Killers* (though even I can't recall why I chose that name). No one else could tell you how many monasteries I visited when much later I wrote a *Wall Street Journal* story about Trappist beers in Belgium. (Five.)

When I write obituaries for the *Wall Street Journal*, family members are almost always eager to talk to me about their departed loved one. Many seem to find it therapeutic.

I am struck by how *much* they care about ensuring their loved one's life will be remembered—and by how *little* they know about that life. Some struggle to answer even the most basic questions. Did she have a middle name? Did he graduate from college? What did he study? What did her parents do for a living? Why did he go to law school and then decide to grow organic onions? How many grandchildren are there?

Most have little or no idea why their loved one chose one path in life over another. Mom or Dad's mission in life has been taken as a given rather than as a puzzle to explore and understand.

A survey of 2,000 British adults in April 2021, sponsored by a lifestory organization called Augr, found that about a third didn't know what their grandparents had done for a living. Two-thirds of the respondents said they would like to know more about their family's history.

My children, should they care, will be able to learn a few things about me—some of it stuff I told them when they weren't listening and some things I never got around to saying.

For instance, they may wonder how I got my names. My parents christened me James Robert Hagerty. The James honored my paternal grandfather. The Robert was for my dad's brother, a navigator in the U.S. Army Air Corps who died in a World War II airplane crash. What my parents always called me, though, was Bob. At some point, in a frivolous attempt to sound like a serious writer, I decided my byline should be James R. Hagerty. Now friends call me Bob, wise guys call me Jim Bob, and other people don't know what to call me. Moral of the story: Name the kid what you intend to call the kid.

As a writer of obituaries, I like to know about people's early jobs, those first steps into adult responsibilities. I've written about successful people who started out fixing radios, parking cars, hustling in pool halls, selling college-lecture notes, or performing magic tricks.

For myself, I will mention my brief teenage job at Kmart, where one day I was assigned to assemble bicycles and then left unsupervised. Pathetically lacking in mechanical skills, I did my best to figure it out. When the first bicycle seemed complete, I found there were still several parts left over whose purpose and place eluded me. I threw them in the trash.

Moral: Be careful where you buy your bike.

I will be sure to write about my few triumphs, such as when, at age 18, I was hired to take publicity photos for a stripper and ended up winning first prize in a local camera club's monthly contest. (More about that later.) But my defeats may be more interesting and instructive.

When I sum up other people's lives, I am not writing tributes. I aim to include the ups and downs, the moments of glory and the flops, sometimes even the humiliations. I must do the same for my own story. But how many of my embarrassing mistakes, lapses, and weaknesses should I record? And which ones? I'm still struggling with that part. It will take time to decide what to include and what to leave unsaid. That's one reason I started early.

So what *have* I been trying to do with my life? From an early age, I wanted to write for a newspaper. Why? I went with the flow. My parents were journalists, and I discovered early on that I had more aptitude for writing than, say, bicycle assembly.

And how has that worked out? Pretty well, on the whole. Journalism has allowed me to test-drive a bulldozer, drink beer with those Trappist monks, and interview a woman who raised 69 children. (More about her later.)

If you count my brief editorship of *Worm Killers*, I've been a journalist for more than sixty years, telling other people's stories and, on rare occasions, my own. I still haven't come up with a better plan.

I HOPE THIS book will inspire you to tell your story and perhaps help other people tell theirs. While we're at it, I will guide you in the art of writing obituaries for those loved ones who refuse to do it for themselves. Whether you are writing your own story or someone else's story, the fundamentals are the same.

When is the best time to get started? Before it's too late. How about right now?

FIRST, LET ME define my terms. By obituary, I mean two things. The first is one of those notices you see in newspapers or on websites. The second is a longer, richer version of your life story, meant for friends and family members, including those not yet born. I believe you should prepare both; one is merely a shorter version of the other.

So is this a book about writing an obituary, or a book about writing a book? In my view, obituaries are almost infinitely expandable. As in life, one thing leads to another. You may start out intending to write only a little, then get carried away and write a lot. My advice is to write as much or as little as you like.

# CHAPTER 2

# Getting Started

THE FIRST STEP IS TO demolish any doubts you may have about this project. So let's deal with those.

You may be wondering: Isn't it morbid?

When they learn that my job is to write obituaries, many people give me a guilty little smirk and say something like, "I know it sounds morbid, but I really *like* reading obituaries."

To me, there is nothing morbid about it. An obituary is a life story, full of sound and fury—plus a few laughs, with any luck, and a lesson or two, signifying something. Death is merely the pretext for telling that story.

> Talking about sex doesn't make you pregnant, and talking about death doesn't make you dead.

Paula Davis, a funeral director in Spokane, Washington, told me she often urges people to write their own obituaries. When people say that's morbid or unpleasant, she makes this point: "Talking about sex doesn't make you pregnant, and talking about death doesn't make you dead."

Okay, but unless you are famous, you may ask: Why should I bother writing my life story? Who would care?

For starters, *you* probably care about it. Chances are you would rather be remembered more or less as you were. You also may want to puncture a few misconceptions about who you were and what you did. You may have a few people to thank for some of the good things that came your way.

Resist the temptation to settle scores, but give your side of the story. The last word and the last laugh can be yours. That should be enough.

There is also a tiny chance that people you've never met will one day be interested in some of what you have to say, if not in you personally. Anne Frank cannot have suspected that the whole world would be fascinated by her story, and would remain so even 75 years after her death. Samuel Pepys, an Englishman who lived from 1633 to 1703 (more about him later), would be forgotten had it not been for his diary, still popular today. It helped, of course, that he was a witness to dramatic events, including the Great Plague of 1665 and the Great Fire of London. But you, too, are a witness of historic events. And what is most important about the stories left by Samuel Pepys and Anne Frank? The sense they give us of day-to-day life in their times.

I'm not suggesting you embark on this project in the hope that one day you will be as famous as Samuel Pepys or Anne Frank. They do, however, set examples that are worth pondering.

Some people have virtually no interest in the past—theirs or anyone else's. In April 2021, Mick Jagger of the Rolling Stones told an interviewer he had tried writing his life story but found the task "all simply dull and upsetting." If Mick could find no satisfaction in reflecting on his past triumphs and misdeeds, then he was wise to move on, tend his gardens, sire more children, or organize another tour. Fans can always turn to Keith Richards's 576-page memoir, *Life*, and learn, for instance, that as a boy he had a pet white mouse named Gladys that he carried to school in his pocket. Note to Mick: Keith also includes a few things about you in his book that you might want to correct.

For some people, writing down a life story will always seem a waste of time. However, if you have read this far into my book, I don't believe you are one of those people. I'm betting you're more like Keith—curious about the past, including your own.

When I am doing research for an obituary, one of my first questions is: Did this person write anything about his or her life? Or record an oral history? Family members often tell me something like this: "Oh, he was too modest to talk about himself!" As if writing down memories is an act of supreme vanity or narcissism. Yet these same family members now want to preserve a proper record of that life—and lack the raw material needed for the story.

Still, you may ask: Do I *deserve* an obituary?

A surprising number of people believe obituaries should be written only about those who were highly successful and/or virtuous. People who want me to write about someone's life often say that so-and-so "surely deserves an obituary." The implication is that others do *not* deserve one. While I am pleased to write about heroic and virtuous deeds, I do not consider them a prerequisite. I'm also curious about the lives of people who were deeply flawed, occasionally monstrous, and often exasperating—in other words, ordinary. To me, our frequent sins, follies, errors, and shortcomings are at least as interesting and instructive as our occasional virtues.

So the question is not whether you deserve to have your story told. It is only whether you want to tell it as only you can.

LET'S PROCEED WITHOUT further doubts.

Of course, we may slam right into another barrier: Many people hate writing and do it only under duress. In this book, I am going to offer advice on how to make writing less stressful and less tiresome. Setting down your story can be enjoyable, at least in small doses.

For those who remain convinced that writing is invariably a form of torture, there is an alternative: telling your story to a recording device. A recording may be less convenient for some of the people you hope to reach with your story, but it does have the advantage of preserving the sound of your voice. It is a perfectly valid alternative or supplement to writing—and what I have to say in this book applies to writers as well as oral historians.

Anyone writing or telling a story must solve the problem of how and where to begin. You could try a literary flourish. You might start with a dramatic event, for example, and then go back to explain what led up to it. You could start at any point in your life and then work forward or backward. You can make things as complicated or simple as you'd like.

Simple is what I tend to like. While it lacks originality, the chronological narrative provides a clear and reliable path for you and your readers or listeners. After you finish your story, you can always go back and rearrange it in any way that suits you. The important thing is to get started in a way that will not require you to stare glumly for hours at a blank computer screen or sheet of paper.

Put down a first sentence—however tentative or drab—and at least you are on your way.

It's best to make a rough outline of the main points you plan to include. To start building an outline, all you need to do is jot down a few notes, a list of topics, in any order. Examples: earliest memories, first friends, family joys and miseries, education, career, romantic entanglements, passions, victories, defeats, lessons learned. Keep this outline handy and add to it as more topics occur to you.

> Put down a first sentence—however tentative or drab—and at least you are on your way.

There is no need to fuss over writing style. Plain and simple will do. Your loved ones will not begrudge you a spelling mistake, a grammatical error, or an awkward phrase. If you crave polish, you can always ask someone to proofread your work and suggest improvements. But first get the whole story on paper.

Now you may well be asking: When will I ever have time for this project?

You will have to schedule time for it.

You may want to schedule occasional writing sessions as brief as 15 or 20 minutes. At a maximum, you probably will not want to devote more than an hour or two at a time to writing your story. If some day you happen to be seized by a fit of energy and enthusiasm that brings out large parts of your story in a gush, don't interrupt the flow. But don't count on that kind of eruption. Writing in short chunks of time allows you to concentrate and avoid the kind of fatigue that may lead to dull and careless language. Pauses between writing sessions allow ideas to bubble to the surface of your mind.

I suggest setting aside one to three short periods each week. For many people, the best time to write is early in the morning, perhaps after a cup of coffee. For night owls or those with odd working hours, a different sort of schedule will impose itself.

When you feel yourself getting drowsy or bored, take a break. The goal is steady progress in small increments, not a forced march.

But where is the finish line? Should you summarize your life story in a few pages or in a book-length text? That is entirely up to you.

For my part, I am writing down almost everything that strikes me as important, instructive, or amusing. Before I cut out the duller parts, my story may sprawl to 50,000 words or more—about the size of this book.

That may strike you as overkill, and you're probably right. But I happen to enjoy writing. I've had a complicated life. There's a lot to explain. For instance, there was that time in 2003 when my boss at the *Wall Street Journal* instructed me to use a company American Express card to order a bottle of penis-enlargement pills. (More on that later.)

After I'm done writing, I will prune out the parts that seem boring or pointless. For the benefit of my children, I will write a very short summary in case they want to pay for a notice in the local newspaper. In writing my longer version for friends and family, however, I'm going to assume that if something interests me, it may interest someone else.

Whether you have roamed the world or spent your whole life in Baraboo, Wisconsin, you almost certainly have lived through dramas and crises, had your joys and miseries, and maybe even accidentally brushed your teeth with Brylcreem. Give yourself time and space to explore it all.

Think way back, to your earliest memories and impressions. The most common error I see in obituaries is to underestimate the importance of childhood and teenage years, and the struggles to find a career, a mate, a vocation, or a purpose in life. Often, these years are omitted entirely or glossed over with a few vague phrases.

The experiences that shaped you are often what other people least understand and would be most interested to know.

In February 2021, the *New York Times* wrote a 2,800-word obituary about Rush Limbaugh, the spouter of countless radio tirades, loved or loathed by Americans depending on their political persuasion and taste in humor. The *Times* recycled some of his most memorable zingers and pondered his effect on elections and the quality of political discourse.

For me, however, the most memorable paragraph from the *Times* obituary was one describing Limbaugh in his youth as "a pudgy loner who disliked school and longed in vain for popularity." He enjoyed listening to the radio and making up play-by-play broadcasts of baseball games. As a teenager, he took a course in radio engineering. After school, he worked as a disc jockey at a local radio station.

Of course, there are many other things to say about Limbaugh's early days, and about yours.

Think about your beginnings. If possible, talk to siblings or old friends to jar loose memories. Consult photo albums, old letters, school yearbooks.

While trying to take a nap one day recently, I remembered an episode from my childhood. I must have been around five years old at the time. My older sisters had both managed to find four-leaf clovers. They pressed these precious charms between the delicate pages of their Bibles for safekeeping.

Oh, how *I* wanted my own four-leaf clover! I must have spent an hour crawling around our back lawn, examining the thousands of sprigs of clover invading our turf. Finally, I got sick of searching for a mutant four-leaf clover and plucked out a standard three-leaf version. I would keep *that* as my talisman. Why did I have to be just like my silly sisters?

Then another problem emerged: I did not have a Bible. Still, I was not to be defeated. I remembered the devotional pamphlets scattered around our house. They contained daily lessons we were supposed to read and discuss before family meals but never did. I snatched up one of these staple-bound volumes and thrust my three-leaf clover between its pages.

This incident could be read two ways: Either I had a pathetic lack of perseverance and ambition. Or I had the wisdom to satisfy myself with what I had.

Some may consider this tale too trivial to include. I'm inclined to throw it in. After all, it's my story.

# CHAPTER 3

# *What to Include:*
# *The Basics*

A LIFE CAN BE ENVISIONED as a mural. You need to step back to see the patterns and possible meanings. At some point, however, you need to zoom back in on the basic details, however dull they may seem.

"It's amazing," one funeral director told me, "when people die and nobody in the family knows which town they were born in."

Some people are more partial to details than others. I always want more. Below are some details I consider mandatory:

**EXACT DATE OF BIRTH:** Day, month, year. If you're worried about identity theft, you can leave the exact date out of the version that will be published online or in the local newspaper. But include it in the family version. If you don't know exactly when people were born, you can't be sure how old they were when they died. The exact date is also useful in genealogical research. It helps distinguish one John Smith from another. Consider

> Some people are more partial to details than others. I always want more.

the needs of your descendants two or three generations hence. Some will be curious about their forebears.

**BIRTH ORDER:** Were you the first, second, or thirteenth child in your family? How you ranked probably had at least some effect on who you turned out to be. Make sure to discuss the influences of your siblings or, if you had none, the experience of being an only child.

**EXACT DATE OF DEATH:** If you're writing your own story, you can leave this detail for someone else to fill in. (I have known people to hazard a guess about when they will die and include it in their own story, but I'm leaving a blank in mine.)

**ORIGINAL FULL NAME, SPELLING OUT ANY MIDDLE NAME(S), AND LATER ALTERATIONS:** Genealogists and family historians will want to know what was on your birth certificate as well as other names you may have been called later. That includes your middle name or names, even if you hated and never used them. Try to explain why your parents chose your name. That is often an interesting tale. Also include any nicknames, explanations for them, and how you felt about them.

**YOUR PARENTS' FULL NAMES, INCLUDING YOUR MOTHER'S MAIDEN NAME.**

**PLACE OF BIRTH AND WHERE YOU GREW UP:** If it was in the U.S., give the city or town as well as the state. If it was outside the U.S., provide enough detail to allow readers to pinpoint the spot. Provide a brief description of the surroundings. As for Grand Forks, North Dakota— not my birthplace, but where I grew up—I will note that the population was around 50,000 and that we were surrounded by incredibly flat fields of wheat, potatoes, and sugar beets in the Red River Valley. Snow sometimes drifted high enough to allow people to climb to their roofs. We had a state university and an Air Force base to bring in outsiders and provide glimmers of the larger world.

**OCCUPATIONS OF PARENTS:** Be as specific as you can be about how your parents or guardians made a living or otherwise occupied their time. If your father was "in sales," explain what he sold and to whom. If your mother was in the steel industry, note the precise nature of her work, whether she was a chief executive or a blast-furnace operator.

**WHAT TYPE OF HOME:** One parent present or two? If your parents divorced or if one died early, discuss the effects on you and your family.

**RELIGION OR LACK OF ONE:** Describe your religious orientation and how that shaped you. If religion was a major influence on your life, it should be a large part of the story you tell.

**OTHER MAJOR INFLUENCES:** Any people, philosophies, or books that guided your life, and why.

**EARLY INTERESTS AND JOBS:** Mine included baseball and delivering newspapers door-to-door. How about yours? The more detail about these life-shaping experiences, the better.

**HOW YOU MET YOUR SPOUSE(S) AND/OR SIGNIFICANT OTHER(S):** Include maiden or birth names, occupations, and educational backgrounds, as well as the specifics of how you met and courted and what caused you to tie or untie any knots, along with dates of marriages and divorces. Describe the effects that romances and emotional entanglements had on your life. Admit your blunders, or at least some of them.

**FULL NAMES AND BIRTH DATES OF YOUR CHILDREN:** Specify whether they are birth children, stepchildren, adopted, or informally designated as your children. You may consider them all simply your kids, but how they got that way is part of the story. Don't forget your pets. I must try to explain my love of dachshunds and describe some of their antics.

**EDUCATIONAL ATTAINMENTS:** This section should include a discussion of why you chose your fields of study and to what extent you found your education helpful or unhelpful in your career and life in general. The social life and friends you found in school may be another important part of the story.

**MILITARY SERVICE:** If you had this experience, it's worth exploring in depth. Not just which branch of service, but where and how you served, unforgettable things that happened, and how military service changed you.

**CAREER PROGRESSION:** Explore how and why you chose your career and how and why it evolved over time. That can be a complicated matter but is worth thinking about and trying to explain. Did you get what you wanted? Describe the highs and lows and lessons learned.

**COMMUNITY INVOLVEMENTS:** Discuss your role at high or low levels in organizations that mattered deeply to you. Explain what attached you to these groups. Include what you achieved or failed to achieve, and why. Mention odd or amusing things that happened. Don't include a long list of groups with which you were involved only briefly or peripherally.

**OUTSIDE INTERESTS, HOBBIES, COLLECTIONS:** Discuss and try to explain how you chose to spend your free time, however meager it may have been, whether it was climbing mountains or watching television. Don't try to get by with generalities like "spending time with family." If spending time with family was one of your priorities, discuss exactly what you did with your family and what you loved and loathed about that.

**CROTCHETS, PET PEEVES, AND QUIRKS:** Do you insist on putting your right shoe on before your left? Do 100 push-ups each morning before breakfast? Consider Chihuahuas adorable? Make sure to include such habits and preferences. Try to explain them.

**FAVORITE STORIES:** Imagine that the person whose story you are telling has just died. Friends and relatives are gathered for a wake. One of them will suddenly brighten up and say, "Remember the time he (fill in the blank)?" or "What about the way she used to (fill in the blank)?" Tell us those stories. They give a precious sense of character and personality.

Don't assume that your family knows all your best stories. I often ask people for favorite stories about a recently departed parent or sibling.

> Don't assume that your family knows all your best stories.

"Oh! There are millions," I am told.

"Great! Just tell me one or two of the best."

At that point, many people draw a blank.

**PHOTOGRAPHS:** As many as possible, including at least one that shows your face clearly. Write down caption information, including who, when, where, and the name of the photographer if possible. It may be obvious to you, but future generations may not know that was Cousin Elmo standing next to you. Try to preserve high-resolution copies of these pictures. If you expect to publish any photo online or in print, make sure you own the image or have permission to use it. Grabbing a photo by an unknown photographer off the internet might create legal liabilities. Don't leave it to friends or family to choose a photo after you die: They might pick one you hate.

# CHAPTER 4

# *What Not to Include*

**ENDORSEMENTS:** Many people believe that an obituary should contain at least three tributes from impressive-sounding people. The trouble with these prepared quotes is that they are too predictable to be interesting and usually too generous to be credible. They waste space and weary the reader needlessly. If you donated a large sum to a school, hospital or a museum, simply state that. You should be proud of it. You don't need a commendation from the beneficiary.

**BOASTS:** Your life story is not a nomination for sainthood. If you won awards and honors, mention them by all means, but consider leaving out marginal ones to avoid tiring or exasperating the reader. It is not the length of your list that counts.

**EXAGGERATIONS:** If you attended a six-week course at Harvard, do not call yourself Harvard-educated.

**THE COMPLETE LIST OF EVERY PUBLIC-SERVICE APPOINTMENT AND CLUB MEMBERSHIP:** Limit yourself to the ones that mattered most. I was on a local economic-advisory committee for eight years but won't mention that because I can't remember any accomplishments and have nothing interesting to report.

**THINGS YOU'RE NOT SURE ABOUT:** You may have the impression that you graduated third in a class of 380, but you may have that wrong. Try to verify. If you can't confirm the information, leave it out. Maybe you'll have to settle for saying you were one of the top-ranked students. If readers find one error in your story, they may have trouble believing the rest.

**THINGS THAT GO WITHOUT SAYING:** Don't describe your spouse as loving unless you see a serious risk readers will doubt that. Likewise for your devotion to your family and attendance at children's and grandchildren's sporting events. If you read obituary pages, you'll find that people are almost always described as devoted to their families and that nothing was more important to them. In most cases, I don't doubt that. But what about people who *loathed* their families? They must live forever because you never read about them on the obituary page.

> Don't describe your spouse as loving unless you see a serious risk readers will doubt that.

CHAPTER 5

# The Telling Details

Oɴᴇ ʀᴇᴀsoɴ ʏoᴜ ᴄᴀɴ ᴛᴇʟʟ your story better than anyone else is that you know the details, not just the broad outlines. The trick is to choose the details that will enliven and illuminate your tale. Reading other people's stories can show you how to do that.

Consider the story of Henry Bloch, a founder of the tax-preparation firm H&R Block. When Bloch died, in 2019, if you had asked friends and family members about the reasons for his success, they probably would have mentioned his optimism and resilience.

We could leave it at that, but it wouldn't be much of a story, not something we would remember the next day.

While working on an obituary about Bloch, I wanted above all to know what *he* had said about his life. Bloch never wrote a memoir but did the next best thing by telling his story to his son Thomas Bloch, who turned it into a book called *Many Happy Returns*.

As a navigator in the U.S. Army Air Corps during World War II, Henry Bloch survived 31 missions over Germany in B-17 bombers, known as Flying Fortresses. After one of those bombing raids, his plane sputtered back to Horham, England, with only one of its four engines still operating. The fuel tank was nearly dry. German fighters shot down scores of his fellow aviators in other planes that day.

One of Bloch's rewards for surviving was to be sent by the Army to Harvard University for training in statistics. While browsing in a Harvard library, he found a 16-page booklet called *Enterprise in Postwar America*, based on a speech by Sumner Huber Slichter, a Harvard economist and informal adviser to President Harry S. Truman. Slichter's booklet inspired 1st Lt. Bloch to think about creating his own firm providing services to the thousands of new companies that would be started by World War II veterans.

After returning to his hometown of Kansas City, Missouri, Bloch drafted an ambitious business plan to supply services in areas including finance, accounting, insurance, and research. When he completed his draft, Bloch wondered what Prof. Slichter would think of the business plan he had inspired. So Bloch boldly requested a meeting with the eminent professor and—in what must have seemed a sign of almost divine favor—promptly secured an appointment to meet Slichter in his Harvard office.

Bloch and his brother Leon set off by train from Kansas City to Boston—more than 1,400 miles, with a change at Penn Station in New York—for their rendezvous with the professor. Surely, the brothers assumed, Slichter would help them perfect their business plan.

When they arrived at Slichter's office, the brothers found that the economist had no time for small talk. He immediately asked for an outline of their business plan.

The professor listened and then gave the Bloch brothers a startling verdict. This is what Henry Bloch recalled hearing: "Most businesses started by veterans will fail—including yours."

This forecast might have crushed another sort of man. Not Henry Bloch, however. The Nazis hadn't managed to shoot him down; Prof. Slichter wouldn't either.

Though Bloch could have found a safe corporate job, he yearned to run his own show and was willing to risk five or ten years of his life in an effort to build a company.

In 1946, Henry and Leon Bloch founded United Business Co. in Kansas City to offer bookkeeping and other services. Their first office was a cubicle subleased from a real estate firm. The brothers began going door-to-door to offer their services to every small business they could find.

Doors slammed in their faces, repeatedly.

Finally, the owner of a hamburger stand hired them to keep his books. Still, business was so slow that Leon gave up in early 1947 and went back to law school. Henry pressed on and eventually was joined by his other brother, Richard.

At one point, Henry became so desperate that he offered to provide bookkeeping services for free to the owner of three gas stations in the hope of proving his worth. A few months later, the gas station owner agreed to pay Henry $45 a month. The business gradually grew, and, among many other things, the Bloch brothers learned to prepare payroll and other tax returns for their small-business clients. They studied Internal Revenue Service booklets and learned how to handle individual tax returns as well.

It was only after nine years, in 1955, that Henry and Richard Bloch concluded that preparing those individual tax returns was by far their best bet. They renamed their company H&R Block. The H was for Henry, the R for Richard. They figured Block was easier to pronounce than Bloch. Thus was born what became the world's largest tax-preparation service.

DAVIDA COADY (1938–2018) also told her own story. And thank goodness for that, because it was an instructive story, and no one else could have made sense of it.

Coady was a physician trained at Columbia University and Harvard. Rather than pursuing riches, she spent more than two decades shuttling, as she put it, from "one human disaster to another," providing medical training and care in Africa, Asia, and Central America.

Meanwhile, her own life was turning into a disaster.

"My pattern was to get drunk and get seduced. I'd sleep with a guy and then get attached to him," she wrote in her memoir, *The Greatest Good.*

Finally, she faced up to her addiction to alcohol and sought aid from Alcoholics Anonymous. Her last alcoholic drink, she wrote, was on October 30, 1989.

If it had been written in haste by someone else, her obituary might have noted in passing that during her travels she met Henry Kissinger, Fidel Castro, and Mother Teresa. And surely that would have impressed readers.

But because Dr. Coady wrote her own story, we know more. Kissinger mixed her a gin and tonic. Mother Teresa held her hand while they conversed. Castro kissed her on the cheek; his beard was surprisingly soft.

THE SIMPLEST WAY to explain how William S. Anderson (1919–2021) found a career would be to say that he met George Haynes, who recommended applying for a job at National Cash Register Co.

The details are more interesting.

Many people owe their careers to people they met in school, at a party, or through some kind of networking. When Anderson met Haynes, the two young men were starving in a prisoner-of-war camp in Hong Kong during World War II. Barely subsisting on small amounts of rice, occasional scraps of meat, and a spinach-like vegetable the prisoners dubbed "green horror," Anderson wasn't certain he would survive long enough to have a career.

When the Japanese military released him in 1945 after nearly four years of misery, he took the suggestion of his friend and applied for work at NCR, based in Dayton, Ohio, a global company at a time when those were rare.

Anderson, born in the Chinese metropolis now known as Wuhan, was cosmopolitan by birth. His father, a Scottish engineer, operated an ice-making plant there. His mother, the daughter of a tea merchant, was half Chinese. When William was six, his father died. As a teenager, he was sent to a British-style school in Shanghai.

As Japanese troops rampaged through China in 1937, he and his mother fled by train to Hong Kong. He found work as an internal auditor at a hotel company. In the evenings, he studied accounting.

Then, in December 1941, Japanese troops invaded Hong Kong. Anderson was a member of the Hong Kong volunteer defense corps, backing up regular British troops. After the Japanese quelled a brief but valiant resistance by the British, Anderson, Haynes, and hundreds of others were imprisoned. The Japanese put them to work improving the runway at Kai Tak Airport. Their tools were picks and shovels.

On a starvation diet, Anderson suffered from swollen feet, fevers, and chronic skin sores. He and other prisoners were shipped at the end of 1943 to a camp in Japan. The passage by sea was no pleasure cruise. "With many cases of dysentery, almost universal seasickness and no toilet facilities, it was a nightmarish scene," Anderson wrote in a 1991 memoir, *Corporate Crisis.* In Japan, the prisoners worked in a factory making locomotives. The guards often beat them. One assault left Anderson's left eye swollen shut for three days.

At one point, the Red Cross delivered packages including tubes of shaving cream. Some of the prisoners were so famished that they ate the shaving cream.

In September 1945, after Japan surrendered, Anderson made his way to London, joined the British branch of National Cash Register, and received sales training before being sent back to Hong Kong to head the company's business there.

In 1947, he was asked to testify at a war crimes trial of prison camp leaders in Japan. During the trial, Anderson identified one of the defendants by the nickname of Fishface. A defense lawyer asked how it was possible that, after 20 months of close proximity, Anderson didn't know the Japanese man's real name. "Well, you see," Anderson recalled replying, "we were never formally introduced."

During that visit to Japan, Anderson happened to meet an American, Janice Robb, who was working as a civilian at the *Pacific Stars and Stripes* newspaper. After their first date, she said later, "he grabbed my datebook and crossed off the names of everyone in there for the next two weeks." Within six weeks, they were married.

Though many Hong Kong merchants still used abacuses rather than cash registers, Anderson persuaded local banks to buy NCR machines. The Hong Kong business grew so successful that in 1959 he was promoted to run NCR's operations in Japan and the rest of Asia. When people asked him how he managed to work with the Japanese after nearly dying in their prison camps, he said he didn't blame the Japanese people in general for the war.

Under Anderson, NCR Japan became one of the company's most profitable offshoots. There was trouble at the company's core, however. Founded in 1884, NCR had grown flabby, bureaucratic, and complacent as the dominant supplier of mechanical cash registers and machines used in accounting and banking. In the 1960s, it underestimated the speed at which microelectronics and computers would turn most of its machines into museum relics.

Alarmed by a loss of sales to more nimble competitors, NCR's board reached across the Pacific in 1972 to appoint Anderson as president of the parent company in Dayton. Within a couple of years, he was chairman and CEO.

With an outsider's disdain for the way things had always been done, Anderson slashed the payroll and invested in new products, including automated teller machines and computers. Profitability recovered, and NCR reported record revenue of $4.07 billion for 1984, the year he retired as chairman.

In retirement, he lived comfortably in California. He was a man of firm habits. Each day, he followed a regime of All-Bran cereal for breakfast, swimming, brisk walks, and a glass of Dewar's whisky, on the rocks, promptly at 7 P.M.

My friend Ken Unico found time during the Covid pandemic to write about some of his greatest misadventures. Ken's children have heard most of his stories, of course, but when he's no longer around they will not be able to recall many of the choicest details. Without details, a story shrivels into oblivion. So here's one of those misadventures as told by the best source, Ken Unico:

> The hardest part of high school in the late 1960s was losing enough weight to make the wrestling team. I entered my first year at Keystone Oaks [in suburban Pittsburgh]

weighing about 110 pounds. The only opening on the varsity wrestling team was in the 88-pound class.

On some level, I knew that crash dieting to reach this remaining weight spot was insane, but I was under pressure from my peers. For the first week, I ate nothing more than a single slice of baloney per day. After that, I limited my intake to one piece of toast each morning. I avoided water because losing water weight seemed the easiest way to shed pounds. My daily liquid supply consisted of four ice cubes.

Soon my entire body was covered with black-and-blue marks. My nose bled every day.

The more weight I lost, the harder it got to lose more. Out of self-preservation, my body's metabolism slowed to a crawl. Muscles not used for wrestling atrophied. Walking up a flight of stairs was exhausting.

Food was all I thought about. I checked my weight 10 times a day.

On Christmas Eve, while everyone was busy opening gifts, I sat at the dining room table eyeballing a plate full of chocolate brownies. The wrestling team was scheduled to compete in a holiday tournament in three days, and I had starved my way to 88 pounds.

Could I afford to eat one brownie? Finally, I stole one from the plate and took it to the bathroom. Stripping down, I stepped onto the scale, holding the forbidden item in hand.

I determined that I could not possibly gain more weight than the few ounces that this brownie weighed. I decided to risk it.

I returned to the dining room table and ate that brownie, one delectable crumb at a time. I savored every morsel as I spread the mini feast out over 40 minutes.

With this done, I once again eyeballed the plate of treats and wondered if I dared afford another.

The decision made by Adam and Eve in the Garden of Eden could not have been tougher. As you may have guessed, I ended up eating every single brownie. Only this time, I devoured them as fast as I could, lest someone try to stop me. Then came the horrible realization of what I had done.

I grabbed a box of Ex-Lax that I had purchased for just such an emergency. After half an hour, it seemed that nothing was happening. So I took more. Eventually I consumed the entire box.

Then I paid the awful price: Vesuvius. My body revolted in unimaginable ways. I found myself butt-glued to the toilet seat for several days. My weight dropped to 86 pounds.

It was all I could do to drag myself onto the mat during the ensuing tournament. I was pinned in the first round.

Ken learned a lesson: For the rest of his high school years, he kept himself very lean but avoided starvation. Why didn't his parents or coach stop him from starving himself? Ken isn't sure. The coach wanted him to fill a lightweight class; his parents apparently assumed that the coach knew what he was doing. Helicopter parenting hadn't been invented. Kids were on their own most of the time. They tended to take their lumps without confiding in Mom or Dad.

Ken believes the ordeal made him tougher and even more determined to succeed—if not at wrestling, at some other sport.

As a student at Duquesne University in Pittsburgh, he tried out for the tennis team. At first he was allowed to join only because he had a car and the other players needed rides to practices and matches. He kept working at his game. As a senior, he was captain of the team.

THE BASIC STORY of the founding of the Friendly's ice cream and family-dining chain is well known: In the summer of 1935, S. Prestley Blake, 21 years old, and his younger brother, Curtis, 18, opened an ice cream shop in Springfield, Massachusetts. That much information can be found on the Friendly's website.

But when I wrote obituaries about the brothers, I wanted to know *why* they decided to make their living by scooping ice cream and frying hamburgers and toasted-cheese sandwiches.

I was in luck: Prestley—known as Pres, pronounced like *press*—took the trouble to write down his story in a 2011 book, *A Friendly Life*. I don't know whether Pres published his story out of vanity or because of a desire to set the record straight and pass along some of his wisdom. I suspect it was a little of both. His motives don't matter. I am grateful to have had a firsthand account.

The real story of Friendly's is more surprising than the official summary. It wasn't the brothers' idea at all. No, the credit for inspiring this splendid business success story goes to their mother, Ethel Blake, a schoolteacher.

In that mid-Depression summer of 1935, neither Pres nor Curt could find a job. They were both college dropouts. When they applied for jobs pumping gas, the gas station owner told them he had more than enough applicants already—and many of them were college graduates.

Mrs. Blake was worried less about the boys' lack of spending money than about the prospect that they would spend their summer wandering the streets and getting in trouble. The Depression, she felt, was no excuse for loafing.

Mrs. Blake had heard about a man in Springfield who had recently begun making ice cream and selling it from his own shop. Her boys, she figured, could do the same. So, with a $547 loan from their parents, Pres and Curt bought a freezer and opened what they called Friendly Ice Cream, furnished with two tables and eight chairs, all purchased used for $8. Pres used a jigsaw to make a wooden sign.

Competitors priced their two-scoop cones at a dime; the Blakes charged a nickel. On their first day in business, July 18, 1935, the temperature soared above 90 degrees Fahrenheit. Customers lined up. First-day receipts totaled $27.61. Their mom kept the books on scraps of cardboard that came with freshly laundered shirts.

Early on, the brothers squabbled about who should do the dishes but managed to patch things up. They expected to be in the ice cream business for only a short time, until something better came along. To survive the first winter, they added hot sandwiches to the menu. The business stumbled along at first but then began growing fast after World War II. Americans were on the move. The Blake brothers offered them good value in a clean restaurant with creamy milkshakes (called Fribbles) and efficient service.

By the late 1970s, they had built a chain of more than 600 family-style restaurants, mostly in New England, New York, and New Jersey. In 1979, they sold the company to Hershey Foods for $162 million.

Pres had a weakness for Rolls-Royce cars and at one point had a fleet of 24 of them at his estate in Somers, Connecticut. (While staying in the Peninsula Hotel in Hong Kong during one of his many world tours, Pres counted only a dozen Rolls-Royces in that establishment's fleet.) To celebrate his 100th birthday, Pres commissioned the construction of a replica of Monticello, Thomas Jefferson's mansion, in Somers.

Pres later donated his Monticello replica to a college. He died in February 2021 at the age of 106, a celebrated entrepreneur and philanthropist. Thanks to his mom.

WHEN DAVID N. DINKINS died in November 2020, the *New York Times* made sure to tell us about his record as mayor of New York. I relished some of the smaller details: He owned four tuxedos, ordered his suits from tailors in Chinatown, and "habitually showered and changed clothes two or three times a day."

In early 2021, I wrote about David Mintz, a caterer and delicatessen owner in New York who invented Tofutti, a non-dairy ice cream made out of tofu. Starting with a dream in the early 1970s, Mintz worked on and off on the project for nine years. One of his experimental mixtures exploded, splattering the ceiling. He finally launched his product in 1981.

Mintz kept tinkering with tofu flavors and textures. "I like a pineapple-sweet-potato Tofutti," he said in 1984, "but the public may not be ready."

One of his hobbies was raising Japanese koi in ponds outside his home in Tenafly, New Jersey. He fed them tofu.

PEOPLE'S PET SAYINGS also are details worth recording. A May 2021 obituary for Clayton Derderian, printed in the *Capital* newspaper of Annapolis, Maryland, informed us that at mealtimes he often announced: "I am not hungry, what's for dessert?"

MANY PEOPLE WANTED to offer me generalizations about the virtues of Richard Robinson (1937–2021), the former chief executive of the Scholastic publishing company. Though heartfelt, those tributes were entirely predictable and hence dull. I was desperate to find a way to depict Robinson in action as he searched for a career. Finally, someone gave me a detailed story that helped illuminate Robinson's personality:

During a break from Harvard in 1957, Robinson and a friend bought a 1941 Cadillac hearse to tour the Rocky Mountains and Pacific Northwest. It had the advantage of plenty of room in back for sleeping. At the end of their adventure, they no longer needed a hearse, and so decided to offer it as a gift to Henry Miller, an author they admired. When they found him at home in Big Sur, California, Miller surprised the young men by declining their offer.

RAY TOMLINSON (1941–2016), a software engineer, helped invent email while working on a precursor of the Internet called ARPANET, a project of a U.S. Defense Department research agency. It was his idea to use the @ sign. When I wrote his obituary, I also included a mention of his remarkable whistling skills. A former colleague recalled watching Tomlinson in the mid-1970s go into a public phone booth and log into the office computer system by whistling a code down the phone line. Tomlinson was, in effect, a human modem.

A RECENT OBITUARY in the *Grand Island Independent* of Nebraska reported that the deceased "enjoyed tinkering and invented many gadgets." To complete this picture, we need to know what some of

YOURS TRULY — 33

those gadgets did, or were supposed to do. Another obituary referred to someone's "unique" sense of humor—and failed to provide a single example of that humor.

ONE OF THE most striking obituaries I have read was that of Sebastian Horsley, who died in 2010 at the age of 47.

Matt Schudel of the *Washington Post* set the tone in his first sentence:

> Sebastian Horsley, an eccentric British dandy who once was crucified in the name of art and whose life of unabashed debauchery and drug addiction caused him to be barred from the United States, died June 17 of a heroin overdose at his home in London.

I have only one quibble with this sparkling sentence: I'm not sure the adjective "eccentric" was necessary.

The *Post* further described Horsley as a journalist and painter, who "led a life of scandal, notoriety and high style." It reported that he sometimes wore velvet suits, fingernail polish, and a stovepipe hat for his strolls through the Soho district of London.

The detail I will always remember, however, was his mock crucifixion in the Philippines in 2000, part of an Easter ritual. After nails pierced his hands, Horsley passed out from the pain. A film of this performance was shown at an exhibition of his paintings.

> If you have ever been crucified, be sure to mention that detail.

The lesson, for writers of life stories, is clear: If you have ever been crucified, be sure to mention that detail.

# CHAPTER 6

# *Questions to Ask*

FIGURING OUT WHAT TO WRITE starts with asking questions.

**THE BASICS:**

What were you trying to achieve in life?

Why?

How did it turn out?

**DRILLING DOWN:**

What are your earliest memories?

What were your favorite toys?

Who were your first friends?

What advice do you remember most from parents, teachers, and friends?

Did you heed that advice? Why or why not?

In what ways did you turn out like or unlike your parents and other family members?

What made you laugh out loud?

What made you cry when you least expected to?

What was it like the first time you fell in love? How did it work out?

If you had a spouse or other life partner, how did you meet?

Why did you stay together or split apart?

What did you learn about getting along with spouses or romantic partners?

If you had children, how did your original ideas about parenting hold up?

Did you have pets?

What made them special?

What set you on the path that led to your career?

Why did you choose that career over other possibilities?

Was it the right choice? Why or why not?

What did you enjoy doing most in your free time and why?

What were the best moments of your life?

What were the worst moments or episodes, and how did you cope with them?

What were the biggest mistakes of your life?

How did you recover from those mistakes, and what did you learn from them?

What advice are you most eager to give to young people?

What are your religious beliefs, if any, and how have they influenced your life?

Do you consider yourself more logical or emotional?

How has your psychological nature affected your life?

What are your superstitions, if any?

What do people misunderstand about you?

What baffles you most about other people?

If you ever have a tombstone, what should it say about
you?

When you're interviewing someone else, here's a good final question: Is there anything else you wanted to say?

# CHAPTER 7

# Interviewing Yourself and Others

IF YOU DECIDE TO WRITE about someone else's life, you will want to interview that person. If you are writing your own story, you will need to ask yourself at least a few questions, and you should consider interviewing friends and family members who can help you understand your story and give you different perspectives on your life and times.

People who have little experience of interviewing may imagine that it is simply a matter of asking questions and writing down the answers. It is more complicated than that, but not so complicated that you can't learn the necessary tricks.

One challenge is to come up with a good list of questions. Think hard: If someone didn't know this person at all, what information and insights would be needed to make sense of the story?

> You almost certainly will overlook some important questions the first time you interview someone. Plan for follow-up chats.

You almost certainly will overlook some important questions the first time you interview someone. Plan for follow-up chats.

You may find that some people give answers that are so vague or hard to understand that they are virtually useless.

Here's a typical exchange between me and someone I am interviewing in order to write an obituary:

*What did your father do for a living?*
He was in sales.

*Sales of what?*
Oh, consumer products.

*What sort of consumer products?*
Household goods.

*Which goods exactly?*
Paper products.

*Napkins and toilet paper?*
Yes.

WHEN I WROTE an obituary about Eula Hall, the founder of a rural Kentucky health clinic (more about her later), I noted that she had early experience selling moonshine. To have written that Eula had worked "in sales" would have been a failure of research.

Be polite, be gentle, but keep asking the question, in different ways, until you get to a satisfactory answer. Ask the same question 10 times in 10 different ways if need be. If you hit an absolute dead end, take a pause and try later or on another day. For some tight-lipped people (such as my dad), it might help to go out for a few drinks. When you hear something that seems worth pursuing further, encourage the flow by saying, "That's interesting. Tell me more."

Be strategic with your list of questions. Don't start with one that may be difficult or unwelcome. Begin with topics that are likely to be comfortable and with questions about good things that have happened. You are helping your subject relax and reassuring him or her

YOURS TRULY — 39

that you are not interested only in the mistakes, errors, and heart-breaks. You want the whole story.

Sometimes people deliberately evade giving you a clear answer because they don't want you to know or write about something. In those cases, you need to keep asking and politely probing until you get as close to the truth as you can.

In my work, I sometimes talk to people for an hour to come up with only a sentence or two of material for my article. If that's what it takes, I consider my time well spent.

Patience! People often meander around a question and tell you many things you weren't seeking and couldn't have imagined. Don't interrupt their digressions; you might learn something important. Let them wander, then go back and gently remind them of the original question they forgot to answer.

Once when I was interviewing an investor in real estate, I asked him about the timing of some event in his early adulthood. He blurted that it happened "after I got out of prison." The interview and story suddenly grew much more complicated, but I was pleased to have stumbled onto a fuller understanding of the man's life.

Sometimes, people let slip their most interesting and frank remarks after you've closed your notebook or turned off your recording device and stopped asking questions. So stay tuned.

AT A BIRTHDAY party in Pittsburgh some years ago, I met Ceinwen King-Smith. She was giving voice lessons to a friend of mine, John Miller, and he had invited her to his party. Most of the people were in their 20s or 30s. Ceinwen was in her late 60s, and she was blind.

A noisy party in a house full of boisterous strangers must be confusing for a blind person, I thought. If so, Ceinwen didn't seem to let that bother her.

As we sat side by side on a sofa, I strained to hear Ceinwen's soft voice. I learned that she spoke Chinese, Russian, and French, among other languages. She had made 23 trips to China.

I would love to know her backstory, I thought, but it was impossible to learn much of it amid the hubbub of the party.

In 2021, while writing this book, I decided to include an interview with someone who wasn't famous but had an interesting life story. Who could be better than Ceinwen?

When you ask Ceinwen a simple question, she tends to give you a complicated answer, with many digressions. Her digressions can be fascinating, so I let her digress. When necessary, I steered her back to the original question.

> An interview should be a leisurely conversation.

An interview should be a leisurely conversation. It should be a mutual exploration, leading to insights for both parties.

We spoke for two hours, in two sessions. Below is an abridged transcript. I hope it will give you a sense of how to interview, or at least how I interview.

*What was your name at birth?*
Ceinwen Klepper.

*How do you pronounce your first name, and what gave your parents the idea for it?*
Kine-Wen. It's a Welsh name from Richard Llewellyn's book *How Green Was My Valley*, which my parents were reading at the time I was born.

*When were you born?*
September 15, 1945. I was born in Chicago but I lived until I was in college in what was then a small nearby community, Prospect Heights, Illinois.

My dad's parents were German. My mom's parents were Lebanese. She was born in Canada, however, and came to the United States when she was nine.

*What did your parents do for a living?*
My dad was a minister of the United Church of Christ. My mother eventually became our associate pastor. My father or-

dained her. In the last few years of her life, she became a kindergarten teacher, and she worked in a school for African American children.

*Do you have any siblings?*
I have one brother, who is 11 years younger. He's a surgeon in Cookeville, Tennessee.

*Did you have sight at birth?*
No. Well, probably not. It's possible I could see for one day. I was born six weeks early and was put in an incubator for a day. It's possible I was blinded by a detachment of the retinas as a result of too much oxygen in the incubator.

*What do you remember about your early days and your discovery you didn't have this thing other people had, sight?*
I always knew that I was blind. It was just a word. It didn't mean much to me. It was sort of an identification thing. And it didn't matter because I went to nursery school and kindergarten with kids who could see.

I remember in kindergarten the kids were supposed to be cutting out pictures from magazines of objects that began with certain letters, and so of course I couldn't do that. So I would run up to the teacher every time I thought of a word that began with that letter, and that is how I had something to do. But I often just played around when kids were doing things like that that I really couldn't participate in.

I enjoyed finger painting. I could make a mess just as well as any other three-year-old.

My first three years of primary school, I went to a school in Chicago that had classes for blind children. We were in a special classroom. We had social studies with the sighted kids. Whenever they had any kind of test we didn't have to do anything. We just sat there. So it wasn't a very good system as far as checking to see if we knew anything.

At recess, the blind kids usually just sat talking in a circle. We weren't allowed to run or do anything. Sometimes we passed a ball around to a little song, but that was the only thing they let us do. Some kids nearby were playing Little Sally Saucer, which is a circle game, where one child is sitting in the middle. You sing a little tune and everybody joins hands and you walk around in a circle. Well, that was a game I could easily play, and I liked playing it.

So I just went to play that game. A teacher grabbed me by the shoulder and shook me like a rag doll and said, "Don't you know you can't play with these children? You're blind! Go over where you belong!"

I got shoved over to the blind kids and had to play passing that boring ball around.

I remember going home and telling my parents, and they were *furious*—not at me, at the teacher.

In fourth grade, I was mainstreamed in our local school before mainstreaming was a word that was even used. From fourth grade on, for the rest of my education, I was in school with sighted people. I never spent much time with blind people.

*As a child did you feel bad about not being sighted?*

No, not usually. When I was in seventh grade, I got picked on a lot at school. People would throw things at me on the playground.

So I learned to seek out the first graders and I would tell them stories during recess, because nobody bothered me if I was with the little kids. And the little kids liked to listen to stories, and I liked to tell them.

When people did things that were unkind, my mother told me, "Just don't react. Just sit there. Don't do anything. Because they want you to react, they want you to get upset, they want you to yell and scream. And if you do nothing, it will be boring for them to torment you, and they'll quit." And they did.

It was difficult, because I'd be screaming inside. But if I didn't do anything outwardly, then the kids would quit picking on me.

*Do you think your parents were pretty good at helping you navigate this situation?*

Yes, they were always very supportive and very loving. I wouldn't trade my childhood and my parents for anything. They let me figure out the things I can't do instead of telling me that I couldn't do things. If there was something I really wanted to do, they usually found a way for me to get it done.

My dad invented all kinds of stuff for me. For example, he got a suitcase and put wheels on the bottom of it and a shelf in the middle so that I could put my braille writer and my typewriter and a couple of books in the suitcase and wheel it around with me.

*Where did you go to middle school and high school?*

I went to public schools in suburban Chicago. My mother felt I needed to live in the sighted world. I feel that I need to adapt to the rest of the world; I do not expect the rest of the world to adapt to me.

There were a few other blind students. One teacher asked me to help some of the other blind kids learn to read braille. I thought that was really cool that she had confidence in me. Those experiences were partly what made me realize that I do believe I'm on this earth to be a teacher. I think my job is to teach, to sing, and to be kind to people. That's what I think I'm here for.

*When did you discover your singing ability?*

My mother tells me I sang my first solo when I was three. I don't remember it. But I always loved to sing.

Mom did a lot of singing, and she also taught piano. She had a few voice students too.

When I was in second grade, she had me go to a blind piano teacher who knew braille.

In school, I was always in choruses and choirs and whatever singing things I could get into.

*What was the popular music that moved you back then?*

We always listened to classical music in the morning when I was getting ready for school. I also remember Patti Page, Rosemary Clooney, Pat Boone maybe.

What I really remember most is the revival of folk music in the early 1960s. Joan Baez, Joni Mitchell...Peter, Paul and Mary...Bob Dylan, Tom Paxton, Woody Guthrie, that type of thing. My first love is really folk music. Folk music and religious music. When I learn a new language, that's really the first thing I want to do, is to learn a song. Songs tell a lot about the culture, and it also helps with pronunciation.

When I was in Nepal, there was one Nepali song that I learned, and I got a lot of mileage out of that because if I sang that, people just melted. It just was a wonderful icebreaker, and people were so pleased that even though I could barely say "Hello, how are you" in Nepali, I could sing this big long song.

*When did you start forming a career plan?*

I think I always wanted to be a teacher. For a while I wanted to be a doctor, when I was little. By the time I was in middle school I realized that maybe being a doctor—and of course for me that meant surgery—was probably not the best thing for a blind person, that might not work too well.

Why did I want to be a doctor? Well, to help people. So maybe I could just be a teacher, and that would take care of my desire to help people.

*What got you interested in foreign languages?*

We always listened to the news on the radio during dinner. They talked about the Russians a lot. And I remember asking Mother, "Do we not like the Russians? What's wrong with them?" And she said, "Well, we don't like the government, we like the people." And that made absolutely no sense to me.

Being a child of the Cold War era, I thought it was very important to get to know the Russians—the people, not just the political system. I wanted to know more about Russian culture, Russian literature, Russian food, Russian music.

I went to an excellent high school. We had Latin, German, French, Spanish, and Russian. I wanted to take Russian. I took a lot of flak because of that; people didn't want me to take Russian.

Russian has an undeserved reputation for being terribly difficult, and it's just because the alphabet is different, and the grammar is really complicated, but it has almost no exceptions, so once you learn a rule, you're done.

I heard about the Russian teacher. Oh! He was terrible! You couldn't chew gum in his class. You couldn't even talk. And I thought, That's my kind of teacher! Oh, yeah, I want to be in that class.

They weren't going to allow me to take Russian, and I said, "Okay, then I will arrange my schedule so that I have a study hall that period and I will audit the Russian class, and I will pass the exam at the end of the year. I'm taking Russian!"

After a few days of the class, the teacher would walk up to me and say, "Ceinwen, do you understand?" And I would say, "Yes." And he would say, "Okay, you explain to the others."

I took three years of Russian in high school, but I got credit for four.

*Where did you go to college?*
Stanford University.

*Why Stanford?*
Because it had a good Russian program. I realized by that time I wanted to major in Russian.

The head of the Russian department told other teachers in the department that I was not to get any A's because she didn't want to encourage me. She said, "What are you going to do with Russian? You can never be a translator because you can't obtain native fluency. And you can never be a teacher because you can't write on a blackboard. And, you know, blind people make beautiful baskets. That's what you should do."

I went home and cried. I was devastated. And then I slept for four hours. When I woke up, I said, "Well, I know that foreign languages are going to be my life's work. If she doesn't like it, that's too bad. I'm just going to disregard her advice, because it was lousy advice, and I'm not going to make baskets. Or at least not for a living."

*What else did you study at Stanford?*
I also studied Chinese. I took Spanish, German, and Russian. I also, of course, had to take the requisite number of literature classes, history of Western civilization, geology. I took a logic class, thinking it would be easy. Oh, my goodness! It almost killed me!

I finished Stanford in three years instead of four. I took a heavy class load.

I graduated sixth in my class, 1966.

While I was there, I met and fell in love with Sandford King-Smith. (Yes, Sandford went to Stanford.) He was in law school at the time. We met in a class in Russian literary criticism. It was way over his head, and so he came to me and asked me for help.

*What did you do after graduating and marrying Sandford?*
We went to Poland. He studied law from the communist point of view. I studied Russian and Chinese, and taught English at a residential school for blind children.

*What town were you in?*
Warsaw.

*And how long did you stay there?*
Eleven months, almost a year.

*And did you enjoy that?*
Oh, yes. We had a wonderful year in Poland. We learned Polish. We had Polish friends.

My main other accomplishment was that I read *War and Peace* in Russian, in braille. It was in 26 volumes.

*What came next?*
We came back to the U.S., and we both went to Harvard. I got my master of arts in teaching in 1968, and my husband got his master's in law.

Then we came to Pittsburgh because he got a job with U.S. Steel, and we were here until 1970.

We had a daughter, Heather, in 1969, the day before the first people landed on the moon. Then we adopted a son, Martin, whose mother was white and whose father was black. His mother was a social worker, and his father was an Army officer, and that's all we know about them.

Martin was five months old when we adopted him.

*Why did you decide to adopt?*
Well, I had always wanted to adopt. I figured there are all these kids around that nobody wants. Why should I go through all that pain when I can have one that's already here? And I never regretted it. He's been a wonderful son.

*Where did you go from Pittsburgh?*
My husband was transferred by U.S. Steel to Port-Cartier, in Quebec. He was a tax attorney.

I hadn't taken math in college, but I ended up teaching seventh-grade math. It was an English-speaking school but a lot of the kids did not speak English well. I said, "Okay, well then I've got to learn French, yesterday." Fortunately, for math you don't need too many words, so I taught math in French.

One day, after I had been teaching for a couple of weeks, I noticed two little boys were playing cards. It's quite obvious when people are playing cards because when they cut the cards it makes a racket. There's no way I would not know they were playing cards.

So I told them to put the cards away, and they didn't.

Later the principal called me into his office, and he said he was going to take the class away from me because these kids were playing cards.

I asked for one more chance. Let me talk to the kids first. He agreed.

I went into the classroom, and I said, "You guys know that two kids were playing cards, and you know that I knew they were playing cards." They said, "Well, we play cards in history all the time."

I said, "The problem is, when you do something bad in someone else's class, it's because you're seventh graders, it's because boys will be boys, there's always some excuse. When it happens in my class, it happens because Mrs. King-Smith is blind and can't see. So, if you want me to not be your teacher anymore, then you keep playing cards. Otherwise, you need to do your math in math class."

After that, we got along really well.

*How long did you stay in Quebec?*

We were there for about a year and a half. Then U.S. Steel transferred my husband to Rio de Janeiro. We spent a year there. I taught seventh-grade math in an American school.

It was hot, oh my gosh it was hot. The people were very nice. We didn't really get too close to anybody. They kind of had their own groups.

Then we came back to Pittsburgh, that would have been in 1973 or 1974. I've been here ever since, with time out for 23 trips to China, 7 trips to Honduras, and a trip to Nepal. All for teaching English.

I taught math in various private schools. The public schools didn't want to hire me. I didn't pass their visual test. I threatened to go to court. It was a long mess. Finally, I was hired to teach English as a second language at a public technical school. I was there for 23 years. Then they closed that school. I ended up at a public school for gifted children. I taught Russian, Chinese, and world culture.

*Could you tell me why you started going to China and why you kept going back?*

I had had a desire to visit China since I was a very small child. One day I was digging a hole with a spoon as a four-year-old and I was told to come in for lunch, and then if I didn't hurry up I would dig all the way to China. I asked my parents if I really could get to China. They said, well, if you dug for a really long time but you'd have to go through the center of the earth and that's pretty hot.

I'm also of the generation that if I didn't eat my food, my mother would say there are people starving in China, and I remember she got very angry with me one day when I pointed out to her that even if I didn't eat it, they couldn't send that food to China anyhow, so I couldn't understand why she was making that parallel, and she got really angry and I couldn't figure out why she was so mad.

So China was sort of always in my thoughts. I started studying the language and got more and more interested in it. A friend at the University of Pittsburgh said she was going to have dinner with 12 Chinese teachers. I ended up inviting them to my house for dinner. And those 12 people ended up actually staying with me for a month, and a couple of them stayed with me for three months. One of them was the head of a foreign language department in Beijing. She arranged for me to go to China in 1986. And I kept coming back because I just love the place, I love the people, I love the food, I love the music. I could probably sing Chinese folk songs for a whole evening.

I flew to China again a few weeks after the Tiananmen Square massacre in June 1989. When I landed in Japan, they told me my flight to Beijing on United Airlines had been canceled. I said, "Well, then put me on the Air China flight." Air China said, "You can't go on this plane because your name isn't on the list." I said, "Well, put it on and then it'll be on the list." And the lady was so shocked that I spoke to her in that way that she put my name on the list.

In China, the customs people were not sure they wanted to let a foreigner into China so soon after the Tiananmen Square events.

My friend said, "Oh, she's not a journalist. She's a friend of China. She even knows Chinese folk songs." And she poked me really hard in the ribs.

And I thought, Okay, this is the time, I have to stand and deliver. And after a 15-hour flight, I was exhausted, I was, you know, wiped out from all the emotional mess of trying to get there in the first place. So I let loose with a Chinese folk song right there in the airport. Everybody dropped their suitcases and stopped to listen to me. The customs people let me in.

*You are really a person who is open to grabbing opportunities.*
If something falls in my lap, why wouldn't I take it?

*You also made seven trips to Honduras. How did that originate?*
I knew a lady who knew a lady who had been instrumental in selling coffee from Honduras in order to help the students there, particularly to help girls get an education. And so she introduced me to this lady, and the lady said, "You've never taught in Honduras, why do you only go to China?" I said, "Well, give me a place to teach and I'll go there." And she did.

*In all of these travels you've had, did there ever come a point where you said, "Traveling is just too difficult for me as a blind person, I've got to give this up."*
That never occurred to me. Why do you have to see to travel? Yeah, sometimes it is possible to get lost on a plane. Actually, it's fairly easy, because if you come out of those washrooms that are in sort of islands in the middle of this huge expanse of seats and if you're not really good at directions you can end up walking down the wrong aisle. I've done that more than once, but somebody will eventually grab me and get me back where I'm supposed to be. You can't get that lost.

And there are people in the airport who help. It's a little daunting sometimes to go someplace where I don't know anybody. I don't know the people I'm going to live with, how are they going to recognize me and, you know, all that kind of thing. Okay, I worry a little bit, but not enough to stop traveling. Look at all the cool stuff I'd miss if I got all flummoxed over the travel.

*Since you retired from the public schools, you've been doing a lot of volunteer teaching of English as a second language for Literacy Pittsburgh. What else have you been doing?*

I'm a member of seven different choirs. I make necklaces. I do a lot of knitting while I'm either tutoring or listening to television or radio. I haven't been making as many cookies. I used to make an awful lot of cookies. I had my personal best with, I think, 57 dozen cookies for the Black and White Summit Against Racism.

Usually, when there's some sort of meeting, I make cookies for it.

Oh, and I do a fair amount of reading. I use the treadmill almost every day.

I don't mind being inside. I'm not an outdoor person. I don't care if the sun shines or not. You know, it doesn't really do much for me.

I've also been editing a 600-page book written by a Chinese author in Canada about life in China just before the Cultural Revolution.

*How long were you married?*

I was married for 11 years. My husband wanted somebody who could learn languages and travel around the world with him. So I fit that bill.

We decided to get divorced before we started hating each other, and I was very fortunate that we managed to stay friends. In fact, I just went to the wedding of his daughter with his second wife. She and I are friends.

If I had it to do over again, I would marry the same guy because we had some good things. I got the experience of going to Canada and Brazil, and I've got two great kids.

*What do you think are the secrets of being a good teacher?*
You've got to know your subject and love your students. If some-
body asks me something I don't know, I just say I don't know and
I find out.

*You grew up in a religious household. Have you always retained your
Christian faith?*
Yes. Church has always been important for me.

I do remember as an 11-year-old asking my mother what
would happen if I decided that I didn't believe in God anymore.
Her answer was, "Well that probably means that your faith is
growing." She didn't freak out over it. I was always encouraged
to question things. I was taught that questioning is how you
grow.

My religion is very rational. I accept science. I don't have any
problem with evolution because that has to do with my physical
body and has nothing to do with my soul. The Bible says God
created man in his own image. Well, God is a spirit. So what did
God create? God created the soul. That's the part of us that's the
image of God.

I don't have all the answers, and we can't understand everything about God. That's kind of a given.

When I was in college, my friends would ask me where was
God when six million Jews were killed. I asked my dad that question. His answer was that God was right there with them. And the
things that happened to them were not God's will. Man has free
will and therefore man can misuse it, and bad things happen.

*You said your mission was to sing and teach and be kind to people. How
has that worked out for you?*
Well, I think that's pretty much what I've done.

*What are your priorities now?*
I guess the same as they've always been. Just keep active, keep
teaching, keep singing as long as I can.

Blindness hasn't kept me from doing things I really want to do, with the possible exception of driving a car. I would love to be able to drive. And, man, if I ever get a self-driving car that I can trust I'm going to give everybody rides everywhere!

CEINWEN HAS GONE quietly about her life as a teacher, never attracting much notice, never seeking it. Ask her a few questions, though, and a rich story emerges. A vital lesson for anyone writing a life story.

CHAPTER 8

# *How to Create an Oral History*

IF YOU CAN'T BEAR THE idea of writing, recording an oral history is a good alternative, whether you're telling someone else's story or your own. It sounds so simple: Just push record and start talking.

The reality, once again, is more complicated. If you are recording another person's story, you generally need to guide the discussion with good interviewing techniques, described in the previous chapter. If you are recording your own story, you might want to ask someone else to interview you. If you are talking solo into your recorder, write a list of topics you want to include, organize your thoughts in advance, and think hard about how to tell your story in a way that makes sense to other people, not just you.

> To avoid fatigue, I suggest recording in sessions of 30 minutes or less.

If you have a lot to say about your life, don't try to say it all at one time. To avoid fatigue, I suggest recording in sessions of 30 minutes or less. Divide your story into episodes and start fresh with each of them.

The project is not satisfactorily completed when you finish talking. At that point, you have only the raw material for a story that needs to be edited if you want to make it interesting and easy to understand.

Type your words into a manuscript, or pay or cajole someone else to do that. (You might also try transcription services, such as Otter, Trint, or Rev.) Then read carefully through the text to eliminate dull passages, correct mistakes, and clarify whatever may not be clear to other people. It helps to have at least one other person read the text and tell you what isn't clear.

You may mention people, places, or organizations in a short-hand form that is clear to you but not to everyone else. UND is a familiar abbreviation for me, but I can't expect other people to know I mean the University of North Dakota. When you mention Fred, it may be obvious to you that you are talking about your uncle; that won't be clear to others. Any jargon you use in your occupation requires translation into plain English. Dates and places should be stated clearly. Provide dates for all major life events, including graduations, weddings, and moves from one employer to another.

If you are interviewing someone for an oral history, remember that you are not there simply to satisfy your personal curiosity. You represent future readers who will not know as much about the context of that person's life and will need more explanations than are normally needed in conversations between people who know each other well.

After you edit the manuscript, save it in paper and digital forms. Make sure your friends and family know where to find it.

You may want to record your edited version in your own voice to make it more personal.

Some people make oral histories on their own, without the benefit of having someone there to ask questions.

Such was the case with Robert B. Greene Sr., the father of Bob Greene, a prolific author and syndicated newspaper columnist. Seven or eight years before he died in 1998, Robert sat down and recorded his oral history on half a dozen cassette tapes in remarkably detailed and vivid terms. These tapes were a surprise gift to Bob and his two siblings.

His father's tapes preserved stories Bob Greene never knew or had half forgotten. They were especially welcome because, as Bob put it, "my father and I had never talked all that easily." They also preserved the sound of Robert's voice.

Robert included the basics: "I was born on March 7, 1915, in Akron, Ohio..." He spoke with pride about his father's having passed the Ohio state bar exam even though he was "a poor boy with only a high school education." Robert recalled his first bicycle rides and the hot chocolate he drank at a drugstore at age four.

After dropping out of college to help support his family, Robert worked as a traveling salesman for Philip Morris cigarettes. Sometimes he handed out free samples at dance halls. "And it was a wonderful thing to see hundreds of young people crowded around the bandstand and listening to Benny Goodman, Gene Krupa, the Dorseys and the like," Robert said in his oral history. "Those days were never to be repeated. But of course, we didn't know that."

In January 1941, he was drafted into the Army, trained, and sent to North Africa and then Italy. He recalled six months of waiting nervously and occasionally fighting along a highway from Florence to Bologna, up and down the Apennine Mountains as the fall of 1944 turned to winter and then spring. "And up and up we went, and in the far distance we could hear artillery fire, and we knew that the Germans were just waiting for us to come around a bend." The dead were put into "white mattress covers" and stacked neatly at road junctions. "The stench was something that one would never forget."

Finally in the spring came "hundreds of trucks bringing German prisoners back from the front....We knew that the war in Italy was going to draw to a close."

Robert came home, settled in Columbus, Ohio, raised a family, and rose to become president of Bron-Shoe Co., which bronzed baby shoes to make family keepsakes.

Near the end of his recordings, Robert said: "I think it's about time to wind this up, but before doing so I think I ought to speak about goals. I really never was goal-oriented. One of my many faults was, and is, my habit, if you will, to ad-lib my way through life, being lucky most of the time to get away with it."

Bob Greene made a transcript of his father's recordings so they would not be lost to future generations lacking cassette-tape players. He also included excerpts from his father's story in a book about Paul Tibbets, pilot of the plane that dropped an atomic bomb on Hiroshima, *Duty: A Father, His Son, and the Man Who Won the War*, published in 2000.

The recordings were almost like a stream of consciousness, Bob told me. He was surprised how well his father, untrained in the art of storytelling, managed to tell his own tale.

Bob and his siblings were grateful for the gift, one that only their father could have given, one that few fathers do give. They were equally thrilled with a written memoir by their mother, Phyllis Greene. Yet they had one regret. "We wished we had been able to interview them," Bob said.

That inspired another book, *To Our Children's Children*, by Bob Greene and his sister, D.G. Fulford. This compact guide lists hundreds of suggested questions to prompt memories and help people figure out which ones to preserve in their life stories. Samples: Do you remember your first kiss? Have you ever had surgery? How would you discipline your grandchildren differently from the way their parents do?

I asked Bob Greene what question he wishes he had asked his parents. He told me there were plenty. The most important, he said, was, "What do you think your life would have been like had the two of you never met?"

That question, Bob said, "would have given them pause; their relationship was so close, they spent so much time together, they enjoyed each other's company so much, that I don't think they ever gave a single thought to what it would have been like to spend their lives without having known each other."

"I'm sure that question would have prompted an initial answer about where they might have lived... things like that. But it wouldn't have taken long for them to realize that the defining joy of their existence—their reason for living—was based on one thing: that they had been a couple for so long."

# CHAPTER 9

# How and Why to Use Humor

Some people believe an obituary can be dignified only if it is also solemn.

I disagree. If an obituary can't be fun, what's the point of dying?

At funerals, you may have noticed, the best moments—those offering relief from sorrow—occur when a eulogist recalls the amusing quirks or humorous sayings and doings of the deceased.

> If an obituary can't be fun, what's the point of dying?

When I ask friends and family members whether they have any favorite stories about a lost loved one, they sometimes reply by saying something like, "Oh, do I ever! But nothing that would be appropriate." They seem to believe that an obituary is not the place for anything silly or any hint of less-than-saintly behavior. Yet our lapses and moments of mirth are a vital part of who we are, or were. If we don't write them down, they vanish.

Michael de Adder, a political cartoonist in Nova Scotia, sat down to write about his mother shortly after she died, in January 2021. As the oldest of her three sons, he took the responsibility of preparing her obituary. The funeral director gave him a deadline, and he had little time to think about the task.

"I'd read a few obituaries," de Adder told me later. "I thought they were rather boring. I thought I'd put a little humor in it."

His opening sentence shattered obituary-writing traditions:

> Margaret Marilyn DeAdder, professional clipper of coupons, baker of cookies, terror behind the wheel, champion of the underdog, ruthless card player, and self-described Queen Bitch, died on Tuesday, January 19, 2021.

He wanted to give a sense of her personality. Though he tried writing some of the sentences in a serious mode, they kept veering off into humor. He couldn't help it. At least, he thought, his brothers would be amused—and then they could delete most of the jokes before publication. In the end, however, his brothers decided the jokes were the perfect way to honor their mom.

The result was an internet sensation, shared millions of times. Here is a condensed version of the rest of the obituary:

> Marilyn, the oldest of four siblings, was born Marilyn Joyce in 1942, to parents Hannah and Edgar Joyce, in New Glasgow [Nova Scotia]. She grew up in a modest home. Growing up with very little taught her how to turn a dime into a dollar, a skill at which she'd excel her whole life.
>
> Marilyn loved all children who weren't her own and loved her own children relative to how clean-shaven they were. She excelled at giving the finger, taking no shit and laughing at jokes, preferably in the shade of blue. She did not excel at suffering fools, hiding her disdain, and putting her car in reverse. A voracious reader, she loved true crime, romance novels and the odd political book.

Trained as a hairdresser before she was married, she was always doing somebody's hair in her kitchen, so much so her kitchen smelled of baking and perm solution. Marilyn had a busy life, but no matter what she was doing she always made time to run her kids' lives as well. Her lifelong hobbies included painting, quilting, baking, gardening, hiking and arson. Marilyn loved tea and toast. The one thing she loved more than tea and toast was reheated tea and toast. She reheated tea by simply turning on the burner, often forgetting about it. She burned many a teapot and caused smoke damage countless times, leaving her kids with the impression that fanning the smoke alarm was a step in brewing tea.

Marilyn liked to volunteer and give back to the community. She was a lifelong volunteer at the Capital Theatre in downtown Moncton, which her sons suspected was her way of seeing all the shows for free. For all of Marilyn's success in life, her crowning achievement occurred in the mid-to-late Eighties, when, left with mounting debt, no job, no car, and no driver's license, she turned it all around to the point in the early Nineties that she had paid down her house, paid cash for all her cars, and got her three boys through university.

Marilyn is survived by her three ungrateful sons, whose names she never got completely right, and whose jokes she didn't completely understand. She loved them very much, even though at least one of them would ruin Christmas every year by coming home with facial hair, and never forgot that one disastrous Christmas in which all three sons showed up with beards. Everything she did, she did for her sons.

Marilyn is survived by her three granddaughters. While her sons committed unspeakable crimes against humanity, her granddaughters could do no wrong. While her sons grew up on root vegetables and powdered milk (funneled directly into the bag to hide the fact that it was powdered, fooling nobody), her granddaughters were fed mountains of sugary snacks as far as the eye could see, including her world-famous cookies and cinnamon rolls. Her love for them was unmatched.

UNLIKE DE ADDER, most people are not professional cartoonists or comedians and would not be inclined, or able, to throw in quite as much hilarity as he did. Many, however, slip in a wry comment or two, if only to puncture any pretense that the deceased was a saint.

A published obituary for Wayne Brockey, a retired wood-plant manager in Klamath Falls, Oregon, was written by one of his grandsons. The first sentence alluded to Brockey's penchant for ordering gadgets and other items touted by TV pitchmen: "QVC lost a loyal customer on Sept. 28, 2016." The obituary also noted that "in retirement, many could describe Wayne as an old grump."

Aaron Brockey, the grandson who wrote the obituary, told me that members of his family are used to joking and teasing one another. He felt it made sense to mention his grandfather's endearing foibles. Terri Holzgang, Brockey's eldest daughter, said her father would have wanted a frank obituary rather than "something more mushy."

I collect these gems of warts-and-all tributes written by family members. Obituaries published in recent years have described deceased relatives variously as cantankerous, grouchy, a demanding old fart, a sore loser, and a pain in the butt. The *Bangor Daily News* in 2008 published a death notice about a woman who had died after "a courageous battle with cancer and a long and aggravating marriage."

A recent *New York Times* death notice, written in advance by the deceased, informed us that she died in her sleep and "was NOT surrounded by her family, since praise the Lord, all her family have jobs."

An obituary for Allen Lee Franklin, who died in a motorcycle accident in Virginia in 2017, described him as "genuine and kind" and also "probably the biggest tightwad in the mid-Atlantic region."

Tony Franklin took on the tough assignment of writing about the death of his brother, Allen, at age 26. The funeral director said the obituary needed to be completed quickly, Tony told me, so "I just wrote it as it came to me."

Among other things, he wrote: "His family constantly warned him about the dangers of riding motorcycles but he was incredibly stubborn. Allen was a wonderful young man and was loved by everyone he met, despite his incessant need to argue with anyone about anything."

When he was writing the obituary, Tony said, he still felt angry at his brother for risking his life on a motorcycle but wanted to capture his personality. "I guess they usually do sort of a generic obituary," Tony said, "but it just didn't seem very fitting for Allen because he wasn't a generic guy."

In life stories, generic will never do.

Kimberly Johnson, a freelance writer in Mooresville, North Carolina, adored her father-in-law, William Wafer, who died in 2016, so she volunteered to write his obituary. Along with his many accomplishments, she recorded for posterity

**In life stories, generic will never do.**

that he could be "raunchy and charmingly vulgar" and "enjoyed his boxed wine from a jelly jar." During meals with polite company, he liked to liven things up by discussing the art of castrating roosters.

Susan Sagan wanted to pay tribute to the sarcastic humor of her son, Noah Altimus of Latrobe, Pennsylvania, after he died of a drug overdose at age 27. "He loved the Pittsburgh Penguins, playing video games, our dog, Lizzy, and chicken," she wrote. "He hated lifting weights, but did it anyway, then had a cigarette."

Lynn Eggers wrote two obituaries for her mother, Rebecca Eggers, who died more than two decades ago in Bemidji, Minnesota. One was serious and traditional, designed to avoid offense. The other said her mother seldom got up early enough to attend her Episcopal church and was "never quiet about her dislike for kitchens and cooking." While attending Sullins College in Virginia, she "learned to smoke and acquired a record number of demerits."

Lynn arranged for both versions to be printed in the Bemidji newspaper but sent only the straight one to Jackson, Tennessee, where her mother grew up. Lynn wasn't sure relatives there would appreciate the humor.

Nate Silver, a lawyer, emailed in May 2021 to tell me that he had already written, provisionally, the first two lines of his obituary: *Nate Silver died yesterday at his home in Bethesda, Maryland, after a long battle with Blue Cross/Blue Shield. He died from complications following surgery for removal of a co-payment.*

"My hope," Nate told me, "is that it won't read, 'At time of death, Mr. Silver was surrounded by members of the Montgomery County SWAT team.'" In any case, Nate has already settled on his epitaph: "He made the best of a bad situation that he himself created."

Ken Fuson (1956–2020), a former reporter for the *Des Moines Register*, made this request in his self-written obituary: "In lieu of flowers, Ken asked that everyone wear black armbands and wail in public during a one-year grieving period. If that doesn't work, how about donating a book to the public libraries in Granger or Indianola?"

WHEN I WROTE about Mother Mary Angelica, a Roman Catholic nun who died in 2016, I described her creation of a religious television, radio, and publishing empire with global reach. I mentioned her impoverished youth in Canton, Ohio, the father who abandoned her, and the mother who suffered from depression.

But no story about Mother Angelica would have been fitting without examples of her wicked sense of humor. It helped make everything else possible.

Her *Mother Angelica Live* TV show had an unpromising concept: A grandmotherly nun sits in an easy chair and discusses religion for an hour in a high-pitched voice. Yet viewers loved her plain talk on matters spiritual and profane. They especially enjoyed her quips.

Her advice to the lovelorn: "People will rave and rant and cry, 'Oh, he left me! I'm going to die.' No, you're not! Just shut up and you'll feel better."

When told during another show about reality TV stars who allowed their intimate acts to be filmed, she asked, "And what do they get for that—besides hellfire?"

Mother Angelica built her empire despite crippling back troubles. In 1956, she promised God she would build a monastery if she could walk after back surgery, according to Raymond Arroyo, her biographer. She managed to do that, but only with the help of crutches and braces. "When you make a deal with God," she concluded, "be very specific."

In 2021, I wrote about Yuan Longping (1930–2021), a revered Chinese agronomist who helped save his country from famine by developing higher-yielding hybrid strains of rice. Most obituaries about Yuan were full of long-winded tributes from agricultural grandees around the world. I preferred to leave those out and concentrate on the many obstacles Yuan faced, including the effects of famine on his own body.

I also found space for the more whimsical side of Yuan, who spoke in an oral history of his early experiments, which included an attempt to graft tomatoes onto sweet potatoes. Yuan said he was "hoping to harvest tomatoes above the ground and potatoes below." Then there was his attempt to cross a watermelon with a pumpkin. His students were amused by the lumpy fruit he produced, which had a "strange and insipid flavor," Yuan reported.

From such unpromising beginnings emerged Yuan's historic advances in rice cultivation.

IT WOULD HAVE been perverse to write about Howard Ruff (1930–2016) in solemn terms and take him too seriously. So I didn't. A born comedian and performer, Ruff was convinced that the world was hurtling toward chaos—and certain that he would profit from whatever disaster engulfed us.

As inflation spiraled in the late 1970s, Ruff became one of America's best-known advocates of preparing for a cataclysm by stocking up on gold, silver, and canned beans. Yet Ruff always rejected the notion that he was a pessimist. "No matter what happens out there, you can create an opportunity," he told the *St. Petersburg Times* in 1988.

Ruff was born into a Mormon family in Berkeley, California. As a boy during World War II, he sang in a patriotic choir called the Victory Boys. "That's when I found what I loved the most in the whole world—applause," he wrote in a 2009 book. He wanted to attend music school, but his mother insisted he follow the Mormon tradition of going on a mission to spread the faith. Knocking on doors in Washington, D.C., for two years taught him how to bounce back from repeated rejection.

At Brigham Young University, he majored in music and minored in economics but dropped out after his junior year. Faced with being drafted into the military, he talked his way into being assigned to a performing unit called the Air Force Singing Sergeants.

After four years in the Air Force, he and his wife, Kay, moved to Denver and bought a local franchise of the Evelyn Wood training program for speed reading. They later acquired the San Francisco Bay Area franchise as well.

The Ruffs became patrons of the Oakland Symphony. He bought her a $1,000 dress so she would look smart in the society pages. Eventually, the Ruffs were caught with too many debts. They filed for bankruptcy in 1968.

Ruff started over, selling nutritional supplements. He also began worrying about the surge of inflation in the 1970s and advocated "emergency food-storage as a kind of family-insurance program." He wrote his first book, the self-published *Famine and Survival in America*. It was "very bad," by the author's own later admission. Still, it led to invitations to share his advice on television and radio programs.

Ditching the nutritional supplements, he launched a newsletter called *Ruff Times* in 1975. Readers learned that they should load up on gold and silver to survive hyperinflation—advice that panned out for a few years. He also began working on *How to Prosper During the Coming Bad Years*, a bestseller he finished in 1978.

His growing celebrity led to a TV talk show, *Ruffhou$e*, daily radio spots, seminars, and conventions where his many disciples gathered. In the early 1980s, he urged followers to buy silver coins, antiques, diamonds, real estate, and freeze-dried food. "We can't avoid runaway inflation and probably a collapse of the economy," he warned cheerfully.

Then things began going terribly wrong: Inflation and interest rates declined. The stock market boomed.

Chastened, Ruff adopted a more positive tone—*Ruff Times* was temporarily renamed *The Financial Success Report*—but he found that happier tidings attracted less attention. As business slowed, he gave up a 20,000-square-foot home with an indoor pool in Mapleton, Utah, and settled into a much smaller house nearby.

Still, Ruff always found something new to sell. His record album, *Howard Ruff Sings,* featured his version of "My Way."

It helped that his wife, Kay, stuck with him. The secret of their enduring marriage, he often said, was that "we're both in love with the same man."

HUMOR ALSO SERVED Gert Boyle (1924–2019) in her business life, as I noted when I wrote her obituary. A Jewish refugee from Nazi Germany, she took over a family business, Columbia Sportswear, in 1970 after her husband died of a heart attack. She and her son, Tim Boyle, transformed a regional maker of ski jackets, fishing vests, and other outerwear into a global company.

Her feisty image proved to be one of Columbia's most valuable assets. The company's ads depicted her as a "tough mother." In one, she displayed a bicep tattoo reading "Born to Nag." Another described her as "obsessive, anal, fanatical. And that's on a good day." A third advised: "If you want something that mellows with age, drink wine."

In her 2005 memoir, she described herself as a "cranky and crotchety old broad" who made sure customers were getting good value.

She deployed her wealth and fame to support the Special Olympics and donated more than $100 million for cancer research at Oregon Health & Science University. She nixed the idea of having a building named after her. "If I'm going to have my name on any cement," she said, "I'll probably be under it."

CHAPTER 10

# *Finding Historical Context*

O~N THE DAY~ I ~WAS~ born in 1956, the world had other news to ponder.

Albert Woolson, age 109, who served as a drummer boy in the Union Army during the Civil War, was in critical condition at a hospital in Duluth, Minnesota. President Dwight D. Eisenhower was sending his Secretary of State, John Foster Dulles, to London for consultations on the Suez Canal crisis. Harold Stassen was trying to persuade the Republican Party to dump Vice President Richard Nixon from the 1956 ticket. Chinese troops were reported to have invaded Burma.

I know all that because I subscribe to Newspapers.com, a service allowing me to search more than 20,000 newspapers dating back to the 18th century. If you don't wish to pay the fees for such a service, you can get access to old newspapers from the reference desks at many public libraries. Internet searches will get you some of the same information, but they are hit or miss for events predating the digital age.

Old newspapers are a good way to find details on events ranging from wars to hurricanes. You might even discover, in a wedding story, a description of the bridal gown worn by your grandmother. I frequently check them for the full names of long-vanished people, products, or companies. You might find surprising or even shocking old news about your relatives. I suggest running a search for articles mentioning you and each of the other major characters in your story.

I often dig into old newspapers to confirm my own memories or things people have told me. Not infrequently I find we were wrong.

Some of the details preserved in old newspapers may astound you. Only a few decades ago, local newspapers included columns recounting news that today would go unmentioned. Here are news items I found in the *Herald and News* of Randolph, Vermont, of November 5, 1925:

> Mrs. Mattie Hutchinson of Hartford was a recent guest of friends in town.
> Miss Lydia Sleeper, who has been ill, is very low.
> The condition of Mrs. James A. Whitney, who is ill, remains about the same.

I RECALL MY mother telling me it was a hot July day in Minneapolis when I was born. Always trust your mother, but verify. The *Minneapolis Morning Tribune* tells me it was rainy, with a high of sixty-three. Good to know.

CHAPTER 11

# *Letters Tell Stories*

CIVILIZED PEOPLE WRITE HOME ONCE a week. My mother told me that when, at age 18, I moved out on my own for university studies and a career. One of my few virtues is that I occasionally heeded my mother's advice or dictates. For decades I wrote to her and my father nearly every week, sometimes more often. My mom saved the letters in two wicker baskets. When I looked through them in early 2021, the letters stacked up to a height of more than two feet.

> Consider writing letters, whether delivered by the postal service, email, or social media.

My parents appreciated the letters. For me, these thousands of old letters gave an unexpected bonus: a record of my life. They serve as an invaluable source of details and incidents I had half-forgotten or sometimes entirely forgotten.

Consider writing letters, whether delivered by the postal service, email, or social media. They will bring joy to someone. Some may also become chapters in your life story.

Writing home regularly was once considered normal, if not compulsory. The children's author Roald Dahl wrote to his mother at least once a week for 32 years, from the time he went to boarding school until her death. His mother saved the letters in neat bundles. They came in handy when Dahl wrote his memoirs.

In writing letters, I had the advantage of being a creature of habit, happy to follow weekly rituals. I also type fast. Writing and storytelling are as natural to me as slicing meat is to a butcher.

Today we mostly send our news in tiny bursts, in the form of emails, texts, or social media postings. Those also can serve as material for a life story, so long as you make sure to preserve the best of them.

If you can find old letters from yourself or others in your circle, mine them for details.

When something interesting happens, write down your memories as soon as possible, without worrying about getting the grammar or literary style exactly right. You might also want to send your note by mail or email to someone, anyone who might appreciate hearing from you. Make someone's day. And save a copy for yourself.

Writing one letter a week can be a good discipline. It forces you to write even when you don't feel that you have anything to say. Sitting down to write has a way of conjuring ideas and events worth recording.

Letters do not require dramatic events or profound thoughts. If you can't think of anything else, write about what you ate for dinner. People who care about you will be interested even in that. Thinking about what you had for dinner, and why, may lead to memories of other events large or small. Tell how you scorched the meat or dropped the toast, and whether it landed jelly side up or down.

Fans of the poet Sylvia Plath (1932–1963) must rejoice in the astonishing number of letters she wrote, including more than 700 to her mother. The first volume of her collected letters, covering 1940 to 1956, runs to nearly 1,400 pages. The second volume fills 1,088 pages. The letters veer from comments on the weather and what she ate for lunch at summer camp to her romances, deepest literary yearnings, giddy hopes, and final despair.

An excerpt from a letter to her mother in December 1954: "if only I get accepted at cambridge! my whole life would explode in a rainbow.... I really think that if I keep working I shall be a good minor writer someday...." She was accepted at Cambridge and by October 1955 reported that she was "beginning to build bridges over some of the whistling voids of my ignorance."

Publication of her poetry in the *New Yorker*, travels in Europe, a fateful encounter at a party with Ted Hughes (who promptly kissed her "bang smash on the mouth"), and suicide at age 30—all these things lay ahead—so much sadness, and yet it would have been even sadder if she had not given us her version of her life.

From the foreword by her daughter, Frieda Hughes: "Through publication of her poems, prose, diaries, and now her collected letters, my mother continues to exist; she is best explained in her own words...."

Snooping into the published letters of E.B. White provides tips for writing from a master, including this one: "I can't pronounce *oeuvre* and the word has never appeared in my corpus, as I am unwilling to use any word I can't pronounce." Note that White thought it was fine to use contractions and didn't mind using the same word twice in one sentence.

The musician Loudon Wainwright III grew up uncomfortably in the shadow of his father, a beloved columnist for *Life* magazine. Loudon II and Loudon III had the strained relationship of wary rivals. Expressing love for his father was "a pretty tall order for me, practically an impossibility," the musician wrote in his memoir, *Liner Notes*. After his father died, Loudon III found a stash of letters his father wrote home during World War II. Those letters helped Loudon III finally appreciate the old man. He wrote a song, "Surviving Twin," dedicated to his dad.

You don't need to be Sylvia Plath, Loudon Wainwright, or E.B. White to write a good letter. Simply use your own voice, as if you were telling a story to a pal.

Whenever something odd happens—the kind of thing you find yourself recounting later to friends—you have material for a letter and perhaps a memory worth saving for your life story. Rereading one of my letters, written in November 1998, when I lived in Atlanta, reminded me of a time when I inherited my father's maroon Oldsmobile. It was unsightly but reliable. I wrote a letter to my mom to explain what happened to that car:

Having your car stolen is highly inconvenient and very expensive but also an adventure.

We were stunned to walk into a downtown parking lot at 7 p.m. Friday and find no sign of the old Olds except for a little pile of glittering window glass on the asphalt. First we called the towing service that hauls away parking violators; they knew nothing of our car. Then we called the police to report that our car had been stolen. A woman told us the car had been taken to A-Tow on Harriet Street, near the federal penitentiary. Before we went there, we would need to go to a police station to get a release form allowing us to reclaim our car.

So we rode the Marta train a few stations and then walked a mile or so down a desolate and dark boulevard. At the police station, a woman did the paperwork and then called a taxi for us. The taxi roared south into parts of Atlanta I had never seen, where shops selling liquor or cashing checks were locked behind huge iron grates.

At A-Tow, behind the cashier's window, sat a man with jug ears and a few greasy strands of hair stretched over his pate like guitar strings. He had a wild look in his eyes and a pistol in his holster.

He said we might want to have a look at the car before paying the $75 fee to reclaim it. We walked into a muddy lot with hundreds of cars in various stages of disintegration. The guard grunted something we couldn't understand about how to find our car. It took about 10 minutes of wandering before we happened upon it. The front was dented into a shallow V. It looked as if someone must have driven straight into a stout signpost or traffic-light pole.

There was a cigarette butt in the ashtray. The seats had been pushed back to about a 45-degree angle so the driver could lounge comfortably. I put the key in the ignition but couldn't turn it. The steering column was all chewed up by someone's hot-wiring maneuver.

So we asked the man with the gun to call a taxi to take us home. On Saturday we dithered. Meanwhile, it rained steadily all day and all night, into the open windows of the old Olds. On Sunday the sun came out and we decided to have another look at the car. Another look convinced me that there might be hope for it.

We asked the A-Tow people to tow our car to Billy's Body & Fender Repair. The tow truck driver was sympathetic: Not long ago someone stole *his* 1984 Cadillac. He told us that most of these thefts are carried out by young guys who just want a joyride. They like old cars. Apparently, old cars are easier to steal.

This morning I talked to Traci at A-Tow. "I can tell you right now it's a total," she snapped. Fixing it would cost at least a few thousand dollars.

If it's too much, we will just have to sell it for scrap. Maybe we'll get $100.

You sure gave us a nice car, Mom. I guess there is no such thing as a free car.

Epilogue: We got nothing for the damned pimpmobile. Billy's Body & Fender Repair was able to mine it for parts, including the four newish tires. I cursed myself for parking the Olds in a street-level lot to save a few bucks, instead of parking it safely in a parking ramp.

# CHAPTER 12

# A Few Words About Writing

A LACK OF PROFESSIONAL WRITING skill is no excuse for failing to tell your life story. You can hire someone else to do it. Better yet, you can do it yourself, in your own voice—and then seek help with editing if you want a bit of polish.

This book is all about getting the story written (or at least recorded). Brilliant writing isn't the point. The point is to preserve your story.

While my purpose is not to tell you how to write, I offer in this chapter a few general writing suggestions.

Before you start writing any section of your story, think about what you're trying to say. Make a few notes about your aims. Maybe go for a walk and think about it. Or lie down for a nap—but bring a notebook to bed because you're apt to think of something before falling asleep.

> Before you start writing any section of your story, think about what you're trying to say.

Make an outline. Your outline can be very rough. It doesn't have to resemble the elaborate constructions, with Roman numerals, numbers, main points, and supporting details, as demanded by some high school English teachers. Before writing a story, I usually find a scrap of paper and list the points that I want to include. Most of these points are summarized with merely a word or two. I list them in any order, as they occur to me.

Then I think about a logical sequence for telling the story and rearrange the list accordingly. I don't worry much about my outline. I know it is only a rough guide. My ideas about how to tell the story will evolve as I write. But this imperfect outline gives me a general roadmap and a start.

Where should you begin your story? As I have already suggested, you might simply begin at the beginning, with your birth, or with a brief note about your ancestors. Later on you might think of an overarching message you would like to place at the beginning of your story. But don't wait until you have found the perfect introduction. Start writing down your story in chronological order. You can rearrange things later if you like.

What kind of tone should you adopt? Try your own conversational voice. You are not writing a thesis, an epic poem, or a legal document.

Keep most of your sentences short and simple. Throw in a few longer ones for variety.

Never use a fancy or bureaucratic word when you can use a simple one.

> BAD: I implemented the rightsizing of our accounting
>    department.
> BETTER: I decided which of my accounting colleagues
>    would get the sack and did my best to ensure they
>    got fair severance pay.

Leave out adjectives that don't add vital information.

> USEFUL ADJECTIVE: pink Corvette.
> NEEDLESS ADJECTIVE: sleek Corvette.

Generally use the active voice.

PASSIVE: I was hired by Exxon to clean up an oil spill.

ACTIVE: Exxon hired me to clean up an oil spill.

Include your favorite anecdotes, the stories you like to tell—that's part of the point!—but don't let your life story become merely a stack of disconnected anecdotes. Weave these vignettes into the bigger story of what you did in life and why. When possible, explain what you learned from each episode, why it was important to you, and what it says about you and your times.

You might ask a friend or family member to read your draft and advise on what should be clarified, what should be expanded, and what should be shrunk or thrown out. You may reject some of the advice, but think it over. Try reading your draft out loud; that will help you find and repair any awkward phrases.

Write as well and vividly as you can, but don't strain to make every sentence witty or epigrammatic. You don't want to wear the reader out with your brilliance. The best writing styles are those that do not call attention to themselves.

Reading well helps you write well. Listening well helps too.

I learned to write mainly because I grew up in a house amply furnished with books, *Life* and *Time* magazines, *Sporting News*, *National Geographic*, and various newspapers. We had only two or three channels on our television set, and most of the time there was nothing worth seeing. If I didn't read, what else was I going to do while eating my Cheerios?

Today you may need to schedule screen-free breaks in secluded spots if you want to read more than a Tweet or a Facebook rant. Still, I don't believe the human race will give up reading. I still find inspiration from books as well as publications including the *Wall Street Journal*, the *New York Times*, the *Economist*, and the *New Yorker*. There are many worthy alternatives.

Turn off the cable-TV shouters. Find a calm and trustworthy writer or podcaster. Listen to *This American Life* instead of talk-radio hotheads.

For more tips on writing, try the venerable *Elements of Style* by William Strunk Jr. and E.B. White or *Simple & Direct* by Jacques Barzun.

# CHAPTER 13

# *Euphemisms: Will You Die, Pass Away, or Transition?*

M<small>Y JOB WRITING OBITUARIES ABOUT</small> other people requires me to spend at least an hour or two a day trolling news websites (including the paid service Factiva and the free Google News) for reports on who has died, anywhere in the world. There must be very few people, anywhere in the world, who read more obituaries than I do.

To begin at the beginning, let us note that most obituaries get off to a bad start. The first sentence almost always tells us that someone has died, even though the headline has already told us that and the article is usually published under the heading of Obituaries, another powerful clue.

Usually, however, we are informed of the death in an oblique manner. There is a curious reluctance to use the word "died," and many recoil even from the conventional euphemism of "passed away."

Here are a few examples of creativity, with names altered to avoid offense.

> The gates of heaven opened, and God's arms welcomed
> Janet into his kingdom.
> After 95 amazing years, Fred started his next adventure.

The final checkered flag was raised for Rachel as she departed her home for an eternally better view of the racetrack.

Harold met Jesus at 8:27 a.m. Wednesday, Oct. 16, 2019. (The specificity of this statement suggests to me that morning is a good time to die because, apparently, there is no line at the pearly gates at that hour.)

Occasionally, people have merely "transitioned." Others, we are told, made a "journey to the Spirit World," were "born into eternal life," left "this world to walk on streets of gold," or "slipped the bonds of earth and soared into heaven to become an Angel."

My advice is to avoid worrying about exactly how to announce that you have passed, soared, plunged, checked out, croaked, kicked the bucket, or otherwise transitioned. By the time they read your story, your family and friends will know you are in a better place. Or maybe a worse place.

So just get on with the story of your life.

Sometimes, however, euphemisms can be useful, especially when you are writing about relatives or friends. As Kay Powell, a former obituary editor for the *Atlanta Journal-Constitution* puts it, "you can be truthful without being hurtful." For instance, Kay told me, "suppose they were a terrible bore. You say, 'He was a raconteur.' That means he was telling stories all the time. People will get the idea."

My obituary will report that I have died. I will not have passed or transitioned, much less soared. I like to keep things simple. But you should use whichever verb you like. After all, it's your obituary.

> Avoid worrying about exactly how to announce that you have passed, soared, plunged, checked out, croaked, kicked the bucket, or otherwise transitioned.

# PART TWO

# *Models and Misfits*

# CHAPTER 14

# A Gallery of Heroes

YOU MEET THE NICEST PEOPLE on the obituary pages.

Some, of course, only *seem* nice because they or their relatives have hushed up the bad stuff they did. Others are genuinely inspirational in some respects, even if deeply flawed in others.

How will you look if your obituary is more or less an honest rendering of your life? It may not be too late to start refashioning the narrative. Reading others' life stories is a way to come up with better ideas for how to live your own life. It also provides a sense of how to write your life story.

Whenever I need to remind myself of a good reason for living, I think of a short book completed in 1946, part memoir, part psychological treatise and guide to living—*Man's Search for Meaning* by Viktor E. Frankl, an Austrian psychiatrist.

Frankl's mother, father, brother, and pregnant wife died in the Holocaust. Frankl himself survived three years in the Auschwitz and Dachau camps.

From his brutal experience came a sublime discovery: Even in the worst situations imaginable, people found meaning in their lives by helping one another endure and rise above their miseries.

Barely alive on watery soup and a single scrap of bread per day, tormented by guards, Frankl discovered meaning and purpose in compassion for his fellow sufferers and in thoughts of his wife. He concluded, "Then I grasped the meaning of the greatest secret that human poetry and human thought and belief have to impart: The salvation of man is through love and in love." This unoriginal but often forgotten insight gave Frankl the strength to carry on.

Being kind to others—including those we don't like, those we feel are unworthy of being liked, and those who have insulted us or let us down—can be considered a self-preserving habit, or even a selfish habit, because *we* are the biggest beneficiaries of our own kindness. Being kind, after all, often requires only small efforts. Yet it is the surest way to feel better about ourselves and the world. It also tends to incline other people toward being kinder to us. We gain more than we give.

IN THIS CHAPTER, I want to introduce you to some of the heroes I've met through my work. None of them are famous. Most of them make me think of how I might improve my own life story, still a work in progress. I have chosen these stories because I hope they will inspire you, too, and give you models of how to live and how to tell stories.

FOR DECADES, FEW people outside Africa knew of Catherine Hamlin (1924–2020) or her mission of medical treatment for women in Ethiopia. Some may have preferred not to know. The wounds she treated were unimaginable to most people in wealthier countries: obstetric fistulas, or holes in the tissue between the birth canal and rectum. These injuries typically occur during prolonged labor, leading to stillbirth, among women in remote areas lacking medical care.

The wounds often turn these women into outcasts, leaking urine or feces through their vaginas.

A network of nonprofit hospitals in Ethiopia, created by Dr. Hamlin and her husband, Reginald Hamlin, treated more than 60,000 Ethiopian women for these wounds over 61 years, according to the Catherine Hamlin Fistula Foundation. The Hamlins' mission—funded by donors in Australia, Canada, and other countries—became widely known in the U.S. in 2004 when Catherine Hamlin appeared on *The Oprah Winfrey Show.*

"If men were getting fistulas," Hamlin remarked during her TV chat with Oprah, "something would have been done years and years ago."

Oprah blurted: "If a man had a hole in his penis? You're darn right about that."

Catherine Hamlin was born Elinor Catherine Nicholson, in Sydney, one of six children. Her father came from a prosperous family, whose interests included the manufacturing of elevators. In a 2001 memoir, *The Hospital by the River,* she described herself as a tomboy who rode horses and climbed trees.

After boarding school, she earned a medical degree at the University of Sydney in 1946. A lecture by a missionary inspired her to find a Christian mission for her medical work. She met a like-minded partner, Reginald Hamlin, at a Sydney women's hospital, where he was the medical superintendent. He was 15 years older. They married when she was 26.

The Hamlins worked as gynecologists and obstetricians in Britain, Hong Kong, and Australia. One day they noticed an advertisement seeking someone to set up a school of midwifery in Addis Ababa, the capital of Ethiopia. Though it was not the most obvious career move, something prompted the Hamlins to say yes. They arrived in 1959. They expected to remain a few years. Then their work, which shifted to a focus on treating fistulas, evolved into a lifetime mission.

"I believe that Reg and I were guided here by God," she wrote.

Settling into Ethiopia was rough. Nights brought the howls of hyenas. The Hamlins drove a secondhand Volkswagen Beetle. They spent much of their time and energy tangling with local bureaucrats.

To learn surgical techniques for fistulas, they wrote to an Egyptian obstetrician and sought advice from other authorities in England and Germany. They eventually developed their own surgical techniques and taught them to other doctors.

Hearing of cures, women traveled hundreds of miles, sometimes on foot, to their hospital. "What a tragic sight they were," Hamlin wrote. "Offensive to smell, dressed in rags, often completely destitute." One woman, after being cured, wanted to kiss the Hamlins' feet.

They befriended and admired the Ethiopian emperor Haile Selassie. After he was deposed, in 1974, the Hamlins endured a long period of violence and political turmoil. Their strategy was to keep a low profile.

"I am sure we were left alone because we were a completely free hospital," she wrote. "As Reg used to say, we were true socialists."

When Reg Hamlin died of cancer, in 1993, Catherine Hamlin was tempted to retire. The hospital gardener took her hand and pleaded, "Don't leave us; we'll all help you." She stayed for the rest of her life and died at her home in Addis Ababa.

UNLIKE MANY CEOs, Cornell Maier (1925–2021) will not be remembered because his name is on a building or program he funded. Instead, he should be remembered as a humble donor who was unusually thoughtful in choosing how to make a difference in his community.

Maier grew up poor in a small South Dakota town and survived 51 bombing missions as a navigator in Europe during World War II. After a mission, B-24 crew members were offered a shot of whiskey to calm their nerves. Maier recalled accepting it only once, after barely making it back to the home base. "We'd been shot up pretty badly," he said, and the fuel was running out.

GI Bill benefits helped him earn an electrical engineering degree at the University of California, Berkeley, in 1949. Maier joined Kaiser Aluminum & Chemical Corp., based in Oakland, California, and stayed at the company for nearly 40 years, 15 of them as chief executive. He retired in the late 1980s.

Then Maier departed from the typical CEO script. Instead of adorning the boards of medical and cultural institutions, he devoted his retirement to hands-on volunteer work at a school for inner-city children and at a children's hospital.

As a donor with strong business credentials, he was invited to join the board of the UCSF Benioff Children's Hospital in Oakland. Maier declined that offer. He preferred to help take care of infants in the hospital's intensive-care unit. Trained volunteers in such units rock babies and provide reassuring human contact when parents are absent and nurses are busy with other work. He showed up for duty two mornings a week for more than 25 years.

"I get so much more out of it than I give," he told the *Oakland Tribune*. "When I'm holding a little baby up on my shoulder, and her warm little cheek is pressing against mine, that's as close to heaven as you can get."

One reason for his success in business, he once said, may have been that he remained single. He could work long hours and accept overseas postings without feeling guilty about the effects on his family.

After retiring, he made time to comfort babies and mentor schoolchildren. "I just think the Good Lord said you'll not have a wife, Cornell, but I'll let you have a lot of children," he said.

EACH WORKDAY MORNING, James Abernathy (1941–2019) put on a starched shirt, a necktie with a tiepin, a three-piece suit, and a fedora. Trailing cigar smoke, he drove a Porsche or Mercedes from his Upper East Side home in Manhattan to his Midtown office.

Panache was part of his image as a co-founder of Abernathy MacGregor, a public-relations firm that specialized in advising CEOs during corporate crises.

Less visible was his other vocation: providing support for addiction-treatment services. A recovered alcoholic who had stopped drinking in 1979, he was a long-serving trustee of the Caron Foundation, a Wernersville, Pennsylvania–based nonprofit that operates alcohol- and drug-addiction treatment centers. In the late 1980s, he and other Caron representatives helped establish similar treatment centers in Russia. He also helped develop such services in Cuba in the 1990s.

Each year, on the anniversary of his attaining sobriety, Abernathy drove to Wernersville to dine with people being treated by the Caron Foundation and tell them the encouraging tale of his experience.

AS THE GRANDSON of one immigrant and the husband of another, I can never resist the life stories of people who have managed to adapt and thrive in a new culture. To me, there is something heroic about nearly all immigrants. One whose story impressed me was Hee Sook Lee (1959–2020).

> I can never resist the life stories of people who have managed to adapt and thrive in a new culture.

She was born in Seoul, where her father was a teacher. After he was paralyzed by a stroke, her mother supported the family by washing dishes and selling mercandise at a flea market. As a teenager, Hee Sook went to work as a waitress. Her mother considered her the most responsible of the four daughters and informed her, "You are the son of the family now."

Hee Sook married a lawyer, Tae Ro Lee, who owned a noodle restaurant in Seoul. In 1989, she moved to Los Angeles with two of their sons. The idea was to stay only a few years. The boys would have an opportunity to perfect their English.

Then the Lees fell in love with Los Angeles and saw business opportunities. The whole family put down roots in California.

Hee Sook founded the BCD Tofu House chain, featuring tofu soup, prepared with a secret combination of spices. At first, business was slow. Hee Sook extended opening hours to accommodate people with odd schedules and those seeking comfort food after a night on the town. She cooked rice in individual portions to order rather than leaving it for long periods to dry out in a rice cooker. She broadened her menu's appeal beyond fans of traditional Korean food by adding optional soup ingredients, including curry, ham, and cheese.

Eventually, there were lines of customers waiting outside her restaurants.

"To succeed in anything, you just have to be fanatically devoted to it," she said.

PAUL POLAK (1933–2019), another immigrant, was a Jewish refugee from Nazi persecution. He became a successful psychiatrist and real estate investor in Denver. Then, when he was in his late 40s, Polak recast himself as what we would now call a social entrepreneur, devoting his business skills to humanitarian projects.

His modest ambition: to eradicate rural poverty from Belize to Bangladesh.

Polak didn't believe that giveaways or subsidies would do the trick. He looked for simple but effective tools that could be sold to poor farmers struggling to survive on tiny plots of land.

Poor people valued and cared for things they had bought, he said. "You can't donate people out of poverty," he said.

The challenge was to figure out which tools were needed and how to make them at an affordable cost. For nearly four decades, Polak roamed the world's poorest regions and quizzed farmers about their needs.

On a visit to Somalia in the early 1980s, he noticed people lugging water and other items by hand or with awkward donkey carts. Working with local blacksmiths, he devised a better donkey cart, using parts from junked automobiles. From that point, he relied on market forces: Blacksmiths began making and selling the carts.

On a larger scale, Polak and colleagues refined designs for foot-powered water pumps, fashioned from sheet metal and bamboo, and drip-irrigation equipment. The irrigation systems were incredibly simple and yet effective. They featured plastic tubing with perforations to let the water dribble out.

He was born in Prachatice, now part of the Czech Republic, and owed his life to his alert father, who noticed refugees arriving from Germany and resolved to flee before it was too late. The Polaks sold almost everything they owned for a pittance, left behind Paul's prized rocking horse, and in 1939 reached Canada, where they were sponsored by a synagogue in Hamilton, Ontario.

As a teenager, Paul created a small business growing strawberries. He earned a medical degree at the University of Western Ontario and completed his residency in psychiatry at the University of Colorado.

While working as a psychiatrist, he invested in apartment buildings and oil-related businesses. In his psychiatric work, he found that poverty afflicted many of his patients. So he began looking for ways to find jobs for them. During a scuba-diving trip to Belize in the 1970s, he hatched an idea to help people process and sell dried fish.

Polak called himself a troublemaker and often criticized mainstream aid providers for being out of touch with local needs. Funds to support his projects came from national aid agencies, the Bill & Melinda Gates Foundation, and the Ford Foundation.

He wrote or co-wrote two books drawing on his experiences, *The Business Solution to Poverty* (2013) and *Out of Poverty* (2008).

His poverty-fighting work spanned Asia, Africa, and Latin America. Polak was modest about his achievements. "One thing led to another," he told NPR. "It was really not very well planned."

LIKE MANY OF US, Ken Behring (1928–2019) also lacked a long-term plan.

In the late 1940s, he rented a muddy field alongside a highway in Monroe, Wisconsin. He thought it would be a good spot for a used-car lot. A former chicken coop served as his office. He had to scrape chicken droppings off the walls before he could paint them.

Behring was so good at selling cars that by 1956 he could afford to begin buying land and developing communities in South Florida. He expanded his wealth in the 1970s by building gated communities near Danville, California, about 30 miles east of San Francisco.

His riches allowed him to buy his own airplanes, hundreds of classic cars, the Seattle Seahawks football team, and a 30,000-square-foot home near Danville inspired by Frank Lloyd Wright's Fallingwater. He caught a 1,050-pound marlin and shot big game in Africa.

What he lacked, according to his 2004 memoir. *Road to Purpose*, was a mission in life. He finally found one by setting up a foundation that eventually provided more than one million wheelchairs to poor people in 155 countries.

Behring had once thought of wheelchairs as a form of confinement, but he found they could be liberating to those who otherwise couldn't move on their own.

Seahawks fans generally hadn't appreciated his efforts to revive their team. Environmentalists denounced his housing projects. People given the gift of mobility, however, sometimes wept with joy.

Behring grew up in Monroe, a small town in Wisconsin's dairy country. His father worked at a lumberyard. His mother cleaned houses and took in laundry. Much of the family's food came from the garden behind their rented house, which lacked hot water.

He remembered his parents as distant and defeated by poverty. "You better develop a personality," his mother told him. "You are not going to make it on your looks."

By age six, he was selling night crawlers for bait. Later, he mowed lawns and carried golf clubs. At age 10, he rose at 4 a.m. to haul milk cans around a cheese plant before school.

The local Montgomery Ward store hired him at 16 to sell sporting goods and paint. If people wanted items not stocked by the store, he found them elsewhere and sold them through his own side business.

He was a star running back on his high school football team, the Cheesemakers. One reason he liked football was that it meant he could have hot showers, not available at home.

A knee injury ended Behring's dream of playing football at the University of Wisconsin. After one semester, he dropped out and went to work as a car salesman. At age 21, he married Patricia Riffle, who had gone to the same high school. Within a few years, he owned his own car dealerships and out-hustled the competition by staying open seven days a week.

After moving to Fort Lauderdale, he began building a home for his family. Before he could finish the house, someone offered to buy it at a price that would give him an instant $10,000 profit. Impressed by the possibilities, he created a construction company and began building condos and single-family homes. In the early 1960s, he developed Tamarac, a town near Fort Lauderdale.

A diversification into prefabricated housing flopped, partly because Behring jumped in without fully understanding the business. Even so, his success as a developer in Florida gave him enough credibility and money to start building gated communities in Northern California.

He funded a training program for inner-city school principals, made major contributions to Smithsonian museums, and helped develop natural history museums in China. At one of his gated communities near Danville, he set up the Blackhawk Museum, featuring classic cars.

In his memoir, Behring recalled lifting a six-year-old Vietnamese girl from a pile of rags and putting her in a new wheelchair. "In that instant, she found hope," he wrote. "For the first time I could remember, I felt joy."

PERHAPS HILDA GIMPEL EISEN (1917–2017) should be remembered for having the last laugh.

In her early 20s, she lost her parents and five siblings to the Holocaust. Hilda survived by fleeing with her husband, David, into a Polish forest, where they joined Jewish resistance forces, sleeping on the ground in rain and snow through two winters.

Near the end of World War II, after her husband died, she pleaded with a Russian military officer to provide an escort so she could visit David's grave. The officer cursed her in the vilest terms and said her husband was lucky that anyone would weep for him. No one would cry for her, the Russian said. So why bother visiting graves?

She later decided the Russian had a point. She had no time for crying. She told herself, "You're going to see what the next day is going to bring."

After the war, she married another Holocaust survivor, Harry Eisen. They moved to Southern California and raised chickens to produce eggs for supermarkets. In their old age, they could afford to donate to Jewish causes. They played cards with other Holocaust survivors.

In the end, the Russian was proved wrong. When Hilda died at the age of 100, there were three children to grieve her, and eight grandchildren, and seven great-grandchildren.

THOSE WHO DIE young rarely leave memoirs. Chris-Tia Donaldson (1979–2021) was an exception, in that and other ways.

A Harvard-educated lawyer, she was starting to succeed in business in 2015 after a long struggle as the founder of a hair-lotion company. Then she was diagnosed with stage two breast cancer. In her 2019 memoir, *This Is Only a Test*, she recalled a moment of rage against her fate. She was tempted to throw her iPhone at the nearest wall but remembered it would be a pain to replace or repair it. Instead, she stomped into her bathroom and kicked the glass shower door Bruce Lee–style.

The door shattered. She curled up and sobbed.

"It was exactly what I needed," she wrote.

As she endured chemotherapy and radiation, Donaldson hung on as CEO of her company, Thank God It's Natural, or tgin, a Chicago-based maker of hair- and skin-care products. The company made potions for Black women, like Donaldson, who wanted a natural hair look. She transformed what had been a tiny home-based business into a supplier to national store chains.

While recovering from those brutal cancer treatments, she created the tgin Foundation to help women who, unlike her, couldn't afford cancer care at the best hospitals.

The company survived. Donaldson died November 13, 2021. She was 42.

In her memoir, she describes an incident that changed the course of her life, long before her cancer diagnosis. Too busy to try to manage her unruly hair, she had begun wearing wigs. While baking teriyaki wings for a party, she leaned too close to the oven and singed the bangs of her wig, turning them into a plastic blob. That's when she finally vowed to "embrace my natural hair, once and for all." It turned into a great business plan.

I recommend her memoir. I also recommend her example of somehow finding time, in a short and busy life, to write her own story.

FAZLE HASAN ABED (1936–2019) was working as a finance executive for Shell Oil in East Pakistan when a cyclone hit the country in 1970. Hundreds of thousands of people died. Abed, a British-educated accountant, felt a duty to organize relief efforts.

Misery was not easily defeated. The next year, the war that transformed East Pakistan into the independent nation of Bangladesh left millions more hungry and adrift. Abed gave up his business career and sold his London apartment, providing funds for him to create the Bangladesh Rehabilitation Assistance Committee, or BRAC, in 1972.

What started as a temporary project turned into a long-term mission. "The death and devastation that I saw happening in my country made my life as an executive in an oil company seem very inconsequential and meaningless," he told the Thomson Reuters Foundation.

BRAC turned into one of the world's largest nongovernmental aid organizations. When Abed died, in 2019, it had 90,000 workers in 11 countries in Asia and Africa. In Bangladesh, it operated nearly 36,000 schools and other educational centers, along with a university serving about 12,000 students.

BRAC funded itself by operating businesses, including a bank making small loans to the poor, a retailer of clothing and housewares, dairy-processing operations, fisheries, a supplier of seeds to farmers, and a maker of recycled paper.

Thinking small wouldn't do, Abed believed. "Small may be beautiful," he often said, "but big is necessary."

He was born in Baniachong, in the Sylhet region of what was then British India. His father was a landowner. As a young man, Abed moved to Glasgow, Scotland, and studied naval architecture for two years. He then moved to London and switched his studies to accounting. While in Britain, he developed an appreciation for Keats, Tennyson, and other English-language poets. In 1968, he returned home to work for Shell.

Working for a global oil company gave him a sense of how to run large organizations, but he still had to learn how to fight poverty. Early on, he noticed that few adults were interested in the literacy and numeracy courses BRAC had set up for them. His conclusion was that BRAC would have to respond to needs identified by those it served rather than telling them what they needed.

In 1973, a BBC broadcast lauded BRAC's fight against poverty and disease. That was helpful, but Abed told BRAC workers that the BBC had focused on the organization's successes without mentioning its lapses. "There is no room for complacency," he said.

One of BRAC's early successes was a campaign to teach mothers how to make an oral-rehydration solution to prevent children from dying of diarrhea. BRAC aimed many of its programs at women. "I have met many defeated men in my life," Abed remarked. "I have never met a defeated woman."

Providing seeds or livestock to people was one of his favorite ways to spur change.

"Poverty is not just poverty of money or income," he said. "We also see a poverty of self-esteem, hope, opportunity, and freedom." Once poor people find themselves able to work their way into a better life, he said, "it's like a light gets turned on."

Though the Bible says the poor will always be with us, Abed did not consider poverty inevitable. "We have called into question the fatalistic belief, prevalent throughout history, that widespread human misery is an immutable part of nature," he said in 2015, when he received the World Food Prize.

EUGENE LANG (1919–2017), a New York entrepreneur living on Fifth Avenue, was invited to his boyhood elementary school in Harlem in 1981 to address the sixth-grade class. He intended to recite the usual platitudes about staying in school and working hard.

At the last moment, he decided that message would not be meaningful—not in such a troubled neighborhood.

Instead, he told the 61 members of the class that he would pay their tuition at a city or state college if they finished high school. He also vowed to stay in touch to help keep them on track.

Thus was born the "I Have a Dream" Foundation, through which wealthy donors continue to mentor and sponsor students.

Lang, the son of a Hungarian immigrant, became far better known for philanthropy than for his business of licensing technology to manufacturers around the world. He ended up donating nearly $200 million to various causes, mostly relating to education.

One reason he could give so much was that he pinched pennies. He refused to ride the Acela express trains when traveling to Washington, D.C. He took an ordinary train or a bus. He bought a sport coat at a closeout sale in the 1950s and was still wearing it half a century later. He chided his daughter for leaving lights on in her home: "It looks like a Christmas tree all lit up!"

Late in his life, a *Wall Street Journal* reporter asked Lang how many honorary degrees he had received for his charitable work. "More than 40 degrees," he said. "Would you like some?"

ROBERT GARDINER (1922–2018), as a 22-year-old U.S. Army officer, crouched in a concrete pillbox atop a hill in Germany's Hürtgen Forest in January 1945. He needed to make a quick decision: Stay put or flee?

Gardiner was born in Denver. His family had a candy business in New York but had moved to Colorado with the hope that cleaner air would help his father, Clement Gardiner, recover from tuberculosis. Clement died when Robert was nine, and the family relocated to a dairy farm near Frederick, Maryland.

At Princeton University, Gardiner majored in history and participated in the Reserve Officers' Training Corps. He wore an Army uniform and marched to classes and meals. At six foot seven, he was conspicuous.

"I remember practicing slouching and bending my knees to appear shorter when measured so that I would qualify for the Army's height limit," he wrote later. After graduating from Princeton in 1943, he was inducted into the Army. In October 1944, he was shipped to Europe. As an artillery forward observer, he wrote, "I served as the eyes of the gunners."

As German troops advanced on that hill in Hürtgen Forest, Gardiner was responsible for directing artillery fire. He stayed at his post, even after mortar fire briefly knocked him out and killed his radio operator. With blood trickling down his back, Gardiner took over the radio duties to provide cover for his troops.

He survived and returned home to launch a career on Wall Street, where nothing ever seemed to fluster him.

Early in his career, he found himself unhappy with his job as an investment analyst at Reynolds & Co. He wrote a letter of resignation.

To Gardiner's surprise, the head of the firm invited him into his office to ask why he was leaving.

"I told him it was a lousy firm, and I told him why it was a lousy firm," Gardiner recalled.

"Instead of throwing me out on my ear, he said, 'Why don't you become my assistant? Maybe we can do something about it.'"

By 1958, he was managing partner of Reynolds as it opened offices across the U.S. and in Canada. Reynolds eventually merged with Dean Witter, which was strong on the West Coast, creating a national firm to rival Merrill Lynch.

Gardiner's optimism was relentless. When the Dow Jones Industrial Average fell 23 percent in one day in October 1987, he assured colleagues it would quickly rebound. (It did.) After he had a stroke on his 89th birthday, doctors didn't expect him to walk again. He regained mobility with help from a walker and enjoyed six more years of shuttling between homes in Gulf Stream, Florida, and Far Hills, New Jersey.

"I like to be in New Jersey when the tulips are blooming," he said. "I'm a big fan of tulips."

SOME ARE REMEMBERED for what they overcame. U.S. Army Air Forces pilot Richard Cooley (1923–2016) woke up in a French hospital in December 1944 and discovered he had lost his right arm in a plane crash.

**Some are remembered for what they overcame.**

He knew he would be all right. "I would make a living," Cooley later wrote. "I would find a wife. I would be happy. But I would probably never play football again." For that, he wept.

Then he moved on.

He graduated from Yale University, became chief executive of Wells Fargo & Co., married four times, taught business at the University of Washington, and excelled at golf, tennis, and squash. He batted up and down the hills of San Francisco in a Mustang with a stick shift. He devised his own technique for tying a necktie. It involved using his left hand, his prosthetic right limb, and his teeth.

Virtually every day of his adult life, he attended Roman Catholic mass. He often declared himself the luckiest man he knew.

Richard Pierce Cooley, the oldest of four children, grew up in the posh New York suburb of Rye. His father headed public relations for New York Bell Telephone. Although the family wasn't rich by Rye standards, they belonged to the Apawamis Club, where young Dick played golf and once met Babe Ruth in the shower room.

Sent to Catholic schools, Cooley learned what he later described as "the consequences of doing sinful things and ending up in hell." At 16, he enrolled in Yale and was a C student, more interested in sports than studies. After struggling in a German class, he looked for a major that didn't have a language requirement. He chose industrial administration and engineering.

His mother barred him from philosophy courses. "She did not want the materialism of Yale to make my religion seem unimportant," he wrote in a 2010 memoir, *Searching Through My Prayer List*.

Playing end on the Yale football team required conquering his "physical fear of the game," he wrote, and "helped me face some of the challenges and obstacles that came later."

World War II interrupted his studies. After pilot training, he was sent to Europe in 1944. During a test flight over France, his P-38 Lightning crashed. Although he managed to parachute to safety, Cooley spent a year recuperating. He later helped train other amputees to ski and otherwise get on with their lives.

ONE OF THE most moving life stories I've written was that of Jean Vanier (1928–2019).

Vanier, who came from a distinguished French-Canadian family, was socially awkward and had trouble deciding what to do with his life. He searched for his vocation in the British and Canadian navies, and later in monasteries, colleges, and seminaries. He finally found it when he befriended two men with severe mental disabilities and invited them to live in his home. His act of kindness grew into an enduring global network of group homes for the disabled, L'Arche International.

Caring for his new friends, feeding and washing them, Vanier found that the benefits flowed both ways. These "misfits of nature," as he put it, taught him to "recognize and accept my own weaknesses and vulnerability. I no longer have to pretend I am strong or clever or better than others."

When I wrote his obituary, my favorite part was something he once told another *Wall Street Journal* writer. My colleague asked Vanier what could be contributed to the betterment of the world by those of us unable or unwilling to devote our entire lives to charity. "Try and find somebody who is lonely," Vanier said. "And when you go to see them, they will see you as the messiah. Go and visit a little old lady who has no friends or family. Bring her flowers. People say, 'But that's nothing.' It is nothing—but it's also everything."

Less than a year after his death came devastating news. Following an investigation, L'Arche International reported findings that Vanier had engaged in "manipulative sexual relationships" with women who were nuns or assistants working in the organization. (None of the women found to have been abused were intellectually disabled, according to the report.)

Vanier's reputation for saintliness was destroyed. And yet, I like to think, not all of his work is invalidated. His life story is still worth knowing.

L'Arche condemned Vanier's misdeeds but pressed on with its mission.

SOME PEOPLE CALLED Eula Hall (1927–2021) a health care hero. Eula said it was simply a matter of being "damn stubborn."

She was born Eula Riley, the second of seven children, on the floor of her family's four-room cabin in Pike County, Kentucky. The cabin lacked electricity and indoor plumbing. Her father was a tenant farmer, and her mother had worked as a schoolteacher.

One of young Eula's early memories, according to *Mud Creek Medicine*, a biography of her by Kiran Bhatraju, was watching her mother nearly bleed to death, in the absence of medical care, while delivering a stillborn child.

As a child, Eula was a dreamer. "I always wanted to be somebody," she said. Because there was no high school near her home, however, she completed her formal education at age 14 and went to work, cooking for coal miners in a boarding house and scrubbing their muddy clothes with a washboard. At 17, she married McKinley Hall, a miner. When he wasn't mining, he made moonshine, with her help. It wasn't rotgut, she specified later. It was "good, clean and safe."

She found her calling by accident. When a neighbor was about to give birth, Eula offered to help her find hospital care. Eula drove the neighbor to one hospital, and then another. They were turned away from both. At a third hospital, Eula gained admission for her friend only after threatening to call the local newspaper.

She began getting a reputation in her new home, Floyd County, Kentucky, for making things happen in circumstances that would defeat others. Later, she publicly confronted an executive of a local hospital company about what she said were hollow promises to serve people who couldn't pay. She berated a school board that shamed children who got subsidized lunches by forcing them to sit apart from their better-off peers. She pushed for a new water-distribution system to reduce reliance on contaminated wells.

Her occupation evolved into social worker, self-taught and unpaid. In need of an income to reduce reliance on an abusive husband, she became a VISTA volunteer in the 1960s—a soldier in President Lyndon Johnson's War on Poverty.

In 1967, the federal Office of Economic Opportunity provided funding for a Floyd County "comprehensive" health-services program. Eula was thrilled with that idea at first but soon became disillusioned. She found that the program often sent patients to hospitals they couldn't afford and was "mostly just a glorified taxi service." Meanwhile, local doctors attacked the program as unfair competition from the feds. Citing mismanagement, the federal agency cut off funding in 1971.

Taking matters into her own hands, Eula set up an informal health service in an old trailer perched on cinder blocks. "I didn't know what the hell I was getting into," she said later.

At first, her Mud Creek Clinic mainly offered advice for people trying to find medical care. Later she attracted young doctors to staff the clinic. Some of the early funding came from a miners' union.

Mary Swaykus worked at the clinic as a family doctor in the mid-1970s. Eula "wanted things done her way," Dr. Swaykus told me. "She was bossy; she was tough; she was absolutely dedicated to bringing health care and legal aid—really, justice—to her neighbors." People with black lung disease, diabetes, and rheumatoid arthritis found help at the clinic. One patient paid his modest fee in the form of cabbage.

Meanwhile, Eula divorced her husband, whom she accused of beating her when he was drunk. The clinic gave her a modest income that allowed her to support herself.

In June 1982, a fire destroyed the clinic. For the first time in decades, Eula cried. She suspected arson. Within days, she was serving patients at a picnic table next to the ruins of her clinic. Soon it moved temporarily into a school lunchroom.

Eula began raising money for a new building by holding yard sales and potluck dinners. Sympathetic police officers looked the other way when she staged roadblocks on a highway to collect donations from passing drivers. A story about her on national television drew donations from faraway admirers. The new clinic opened in 1984.

In a 1987 interview with the *Louisville Courier-Journal*, Eula spoke of the challenges of attracting doctors to work for low salaries in a rural area. "Ain't nothing here but hard work and sick people," she said. On the other hand, she added, advice and preventive medicine went a long way: "What we do is we keep little problems from becoming major problems."

AUGUST DE LOS REYES (1970–2020) fell out of bed and found a mission.

In 2013, Microsoft gave de los Reyes his dream job—overseeing design for Xbox game consoles. Around the same time, he read an article about how to sleep better and "really geeked out on bedding," as he put it in a podcast. De los Reyes purchased a down comforter so enormous that it "created a misperception of how big my bed was." One day, aiming to ease back onto that cloud of softness, he misjudged the dimensions of the bed, fell, and slammed his back against a bed rail. He was left paralyzed from the chest down.

This disaster, he concluded later, made him a better product designer. He devoted the rest of his career to finding people whose disabilities excluded them from an activity and then making things work for them.

That sort of design, he discovered, could help all of us, not just the excluded few. One example: the remote control. It was initially designed for people unable to get off the sofa to change the TV channel. Now almost everyone uses it.

"If you solve for one," De los Reyes liked to say, "it will benefit many." His aim was "to be a kind of Johnny Appleseed in spreading this approach to design and accessibility." He opposed designing for "the so-called average consumer, which doesn't even exist."

Writing isn't the only option for telling your story.

He was just 50 years old when he died in December 2020 of COVID-19. He was survived by his husband, Rein Ewerth, and a cat named Salad.

De los Reyes didn't write a memoir. He did leave behind a podcast that told much of his story in his own words. Writing isn't the only option for telling your story.

WHEN JOYCE DUMONT dies, it will be hard—maybe impossible—to compile a list of all her survivors. It may be best merely to state that she is survived by multitudes. There is no doubt she will be remembered fondly.

Joyce is a retired nurse and a Native American of the Chippewa tribe who lives in the small town of Dunseith, North Dakota, near the International Peace Garden on the Canadian border. When I met

Joyce in 2013, she had helped raise 69 kids—including six through childbirth, five stepchildren, eleven who were adopted, several dozen foster children, and a few who simply moved in when they had no better place to go.

Joyce didn't consider herself extraordinary. She never sought publicity or entertained the idea that her story might interest anyone. Her renown spread beyond Dunseith only because Joyce happened to meet my mother at an Adoption Day celebration in 2011, and my mom wrote about her in the North Dakota *Grand Forks Herald*. In 2013, Joyce was on page one of the *Wall Street Journal* when I told her story. *People* magazine published a similar story about Joyce in 2015.

Her debut as a mom was rocky. When she graduated from high school, she told me, "I was 18 years old, and I thought I was really smart, so I decided to marry this guy." She and her first husband had six children together. They roamed the country from Illinois to California, but the marriage broke down back in North Dakota.

While he was away for a few days, she says, she hired a moving crew to uproot the entire house and haul it to a plot in another part of Dunseith, a town of about 800 people. When her husband returned, he found only the front steps where the family home had stood. The message was clear. Divorce ensued.

As a single mom in the late 1960s, she worked as a teacher's aide by day and restaurant cook by night. "Sometimes, boy, it got really slim," she said of the family budget. Her eldest son, Rocky Davis, helped care for his brothers and sisters. "We learned how to cook early," Rocky said. He remembered being "basically the dad of the house."

Joyce had to earn a living. She obtained a state grant to pay for nursing school. Around that time, she met a divorced truck driver who was raising two children. At first she was reluctant to date him. He won her over by saying, "Let's go to the movies with the kids." They married in 1970 and were together till he died of cancer 32 years later.

Her brood kept growing. It was not by design. Joyce was merely responding in her own way to circumstances. She lived in an area blighted by poverty and alcoholism.

Having noticed her generosity, social workers regularly asked her to take in foster children. She volunteered to shelter others after hearing they were in trouble. Some simply showed up. A high-school buddy of one of her stepsons was invited for a sleepover in the late 1970s and stayed two years.

At the very least, visitors to her house were expected to stay for a meal, often of what she calls Indian tacos, made from deep-fried bread dough, hamburger, sour cream, raw onions, tomatoes, and black olives.

When I visited, she was living in a one-story beige house on a hillside surrounded by oak and birch trees. There were three small bedrooms, along with two beds in the living room and more in the basement to handle the occasional overflow. In one corner of her living room, rainwater had leaked through a ceiling panel. "My roof busted in," Joyce explained cheerfully. "I had a pail there."

A washing machine was chugging, and a chubby Chihuahua named Peewee scoured the floor for Cheerios.

As a parent, her style was to demonstrate rather than shout. When she found one boy's stash of marijuana, she flushed it down a toilet. Her tears could stop a sibling squabble. After a daughter sneaked out of middle school, Joyce took her hand and silently led her back, then sat next to her all through typing class. That daughter, Marilyn Ruberry, told me the incident was so embarrassing that she never skipped school again. She grew up to be a bookkeeper in Raymond, Alberta.

"All children want is something stable," Joyce told me. "They want to know that you love them. It doesn't have to be love with big computers and fancy clothes and all of that. Just that you care."

# CHAPTER 15

# *A Gallery of Characters*

IT IS NOT ONLY BY our acts of kindness, large or small, that we may be fondly remembered. Our friends and families also will cherish our originality, strange habits, lost causes, baffling behaviors, obsessions, quirks, and general cussedness.

In this chapter, I present some of the most memorable characters I have encountered on the obituary beat. My goal is to suggest ways to recognize individual traits worth remembering and preserve them in words.

> Our friends and families also will cherish our originality, strange habits, lost causes, baffling behaviors, obsessions, quirks, and general cussedness.

PEOPLE WHO ARE sticklers for correct punctuation may want to celebrate John Richards (1923–2021).

After a career as a newspaper reporter and editor in England, Richards took it upon himself to defend the apostrophe. When he started the Apostrophe Protection Society, in 2001, there were only two members, Richards and his son, Stephen. Soon, however, he had more than 250 members. Some made unsolicited cash donations.

Letters and emails, arriving from all over, bore witness to flagrant examples of misuse of the apostrophe. Many offenders left the apostrophe out of possessive phrases. Others inserted the mark where it wasn't needed, as in market signs advertising "apple's."

Not everyone shared his concern. Richards told the *Daily Mail* that he spotted a restaurant advertising "coffee's." He offered free advice. "I said very politely, 'It's not needed. It's a plural,'" Richards said. "But the man said, 'I think it looks better with an apostrophe.' And what can you say to that?"

In defending the apostrophe, he tried to avoid hectoring or insulting anyone. His typical letter of advice opened like this: "Dear Sir or Madam, Because there seems to be some doubt about the use of the apostrophe, we are taking the liberty of drawing your attention to an incorrect use."

He chose his battles, rather than taking on all abuses of grammar and usage. In a 2001 interview with the *New York Times*, he said: "The incorrect use of 'fewer' and 'less' is another thing that annoys me. If I carry on, I'll get quite worked up."

Richards was no fanatic. He accepted the natural evolution of language. "Of course English is changing," he told the *Washington Post* in 2009. "If the change is an improvement, yes, that's fine. I think a lot of the change now is due to laziness and ignorance. It's going downhill."

His battle was uphill. In 2019, he finally shut down his campaign. "The barbarians," he declared, "have won."

By then, Richards had evolved. "I'm just not as enthusiastic as I was," he said. "I think it may be an age thing, but somehow the apostrophe doesn't seem to matter to me as much as it did."

DUVALL HECHT (1930–2022) was a master of reinvention. Raised in Los Angeles as the son of a stockbroker, he enrolled in Stanford University to study journalism and discovered something far more exciting—crew racing as a member of the rowing team. Later, while serving as a fighter pilot in the U.S. Marines, he continued to row and qualified for the 1952 and 1956 Olympics. At the 1956 Olympics in

Melbourne, he and a pal, Jim Fifer, sprinted past their Russian rivals to win gold medals in the pair-without-coxswain races.

Hecht briefly taught English at Menlo College and then became a marketing manager at a securities firm in Los Angeles. During his commutes to work in the early 1970s, he found himself sick of listening to what he called "bad music and worse news." So he propped a reel-to-reel tape player on the passenger seat and listened to books for the blind.

That awkward arrangement sparked a business idea: recording books on cassette tapes, which were becoming popular in the 1970s as more people had tape players installed in their cars. In 1975, Hecht founded Books on Tape Inc. He raised seed money by selling his 10-year-old Porsche.

He was about a decade ahead of the rush by big publishers to promote abridged bestsellers, sometimes read by big-name actors. Hecht had a different approach: He preferred unabridged books, even if that meant several dozen tapes for *War and Peace*. He hired little-known actors. They charged less and tended not to distract the reader with stagy vocal flourishes.

"We have weavers and sculptors who rent from us," Mr. Hecht told the *Wall Street Journal* in 1986. "There's even an undertaker who listens with a tiny earpiece during funerals."

Though his firm never became a giant, it employed dozens of people in Costa Mesa, California, and had steady demand from libraries and people who wanted to hear the whole book. Hecht could afford to buy a new Porsche. His license plate read LSN2BKS.

In 2001, he sold the firm to Bertelsmann's Random House unit for an estimated $20 million.

He was in his early 70s and uninterested in retirement. After finding employers reluctant to hire a man of his age, Hecht reverted to one of his boyhood fantasies: driving a long-haul truck. A six-month course qualified him to work for a haulage company. He soon bought his own Freightliner truck. His truck-driving career lasted seven years.

Driving a truck "is my meditation," he told the *Orange County Business Journal*. "It's solitude. You can hardly find that anymore."

There was another benefit: He had more time to listen to books.

EARL GRAVES (1935–2020), the son of an immigrant from Barbados, grew up in the Bedford-Stuyvesant neighborhood of Brooklyn. As a student at what is now Morgan State University in Baltimore in the 1950s, he needed cash and decided to start a lawn-mowing service.

"Your gardening worries are over!" he announced in a mimeographed flier. "Stop breaking your back."

There was a problem, though: Graves didn't have a phone. How were potential customers going to reach him? Simple: His ad listed the phone number of the university's main office. That worked fine until a dean discovered that a mowing service was relying on the school's secretarial pool.

"He couldn't believe my nerve," Graves later told *Crain's New York Business*.

His nerve ended up serving him well. Graves founded *Black Enterprise* magazine in 1970 and ran a Pepsi-Cola bottling business in Washington, D.C., in the 1990s. He became a director of companies including Aetna, Chrysler, and Federated Department Stores. He wrote a popular 1997 book called *How to Succeed in Business Without Being White.*

Graves wore elegant suits and kept his mutton-chop sideburns carefully trimmed. With his wife, Barbara, he raised three sons in a 10-bedroom home in Scarsdale, New York. It had a 60-foot swimming pool, a tennis court, and an ice-cream parlor. The sons graduated from Yale, Brown, and the University of Pennsylvania.

Graves gave credit to his father, a shipping clerk in a garment factory, for instilling a work ethic in him. "I swept the sidewalk once a day and God forbid if I didn't bring the garbage cans in after the garbage had been collected," he told the *Los Angeles Times*. He also credited his wife for helping him launch and manage *Black Enterprise*. She was "vice president in charge of shutting down the publisher's bad ideas," he wrote.

He made large donations to Morgan State, which named its business school and an honors program after him.

Graves denounced racism but also chided Black people for not doing more to help one another. "Some Black people, given a choice between buying ice from a Black man or a white man, will pick the white man, because they actually believe that the white man's ice is colder," he said in a 1997 speech.

Graves often looked back to his formative years at Morgan State. "I may have been the slowest man ever to have a place on the Morgan State track team," he wrote, "but when it came to running after money, I was an Olympian."

CLAYTON M. CHRISTENSEN (1952–2020), a Harvard Business School professor and management guru, was an authority on disruptive technologies, those that allow newcomers to swoop into a business and defeat the incumbents. He became more widely known, however, for offering his own life as a case study.

In a 2010 article and lecture—entitled "How Will You Measure Your Life?," and later expanded into a book that was later expanded into a book—he advised business-school students to devote some of their time to creating a strategy for living a good life. Having a clear purpose mattered more than mastering core competences and disruptive innovations, he argued.

A lifelong member of the Church of Jesus Christ of Latter-day Saints, he spoke of a tough decision he made while playing basketball for a team at Oxford University. He outraged teammates by refusing to participate in a championship game on a Sunday. "Had I crossed the line that one time, I would have done it over and over in the years that followed," he wrote.

As a consultant and professor, Christensen saw his role as telling people how to think rather than what to do. He urged students to look beyond profit margins and near-term results.

"More and more MBA students come to school thinking that a career in business means buying, selling, and investing in companies," he wrote. "That's unfortunate. Doing deals doesn't yield the deep rewards that come from building up people."

Though Christensen put his faith at the center of his messages, he said his prescriptions for leading a successful life applied to everyone.

He was born Clayton Magleby Christensen, the second of eight children of a family in Salt Lake City. His father managed the grocery section of a department store. His mother was a high school English teacher and wrote for radio programs.

In sixth grade, he read the entire *World Book Encyclopedia*, according to his family. Around the same age, he became a regular reader of the *Congressional Record* and made charts of the voting records of members of Congress. One of his early ambitions was to become editor of the *Wall Street Journal*.

Standing six foot eight, he played basketball in high school and college. Following the tradition of his church, he worked as a missionary in South Korea in the early 1970s.

Branding could apply to families as well as goods and services, he believed. When one of his children was accused of pushing another student at school, Christensen convened a family meeting. "The brand is that the Christensens are known for kindness," he announced.

He expected that brand to serve him well in the afterlife. "When I pass on and have my interview with God, he is not going to say, 'Oh my gosh, Clay Christensen, you were a famous professor at H.B.S.,'" Christensen told the *Wall Street Journal* in 2016. "He's going to say, 'Can we just talk about the individual people you helped become better people?'"

CHET CUNNINGHAM (1928–2017) was known for persistence in his chosen trade and for not obsessing over what other people thought of his work.

When Cunningham submitted a novel in 1972, he got a letter back from a publisher, Pinnacle Books. "While this is not the best Western I've ever read," an editor wrote, "we've decided to publish it."

That was good enough for Cunningham. He had three children and a wife suffering from multiple sclerosis. He needed income. By his own count, over nearly five decades, he produced 375 published books, including Westerns, thrillers, a motorcycle-maintenance manual, and handbooks for sufferers of sciatica and irritable bowel syndrome. Sometimes he wrote romance novels under a pseudonym, Cathy Cunningham.

"He pretty much wrote whatever somebody would pay him for," said Greg Cunningham, his son.

He didn't wait around for inspiration to strike. "A carpenter doesn't not go into work because he has carpenter's block," said his daughter, Christine Ashworth, also a novelist. "He considered writing a craft, and he just did it."

Cunningham's books typically take readers directly to the action, with no detours for flowery description or philosophical musing. The first sentence of his novel *Vengeance Mine* reads, "Assistant Manager Roger Hornsake had just locked the front door and closed the blinds of the San Diego Trust bank when a gunman pushed a revolver into his back."

In the opening scene of another Cunningham novel, *Scream Vengeance*, Detective Stacy DeFrain examines a corpse. "This is totally weird," she says. "It could have been a suicide if her hands weren't tied behind her back and her ankles not tied together with panty hose."

Cunningham did his writing at home in a converted bedroom, where he was surrounded by filing cabinets and thousands of books. "Walk down the hall, turn left, and I'm at work," he said.

His full name was Chester Grant Cunningham. He was born December 9, 1928, in Shelby, Nebraska. His parents, who farmed near Shelby, were "blown out of Nebraska in 1937 by the Dust Bowl," he wrote. The family relocated to Forest Grove, Oregon. Chet's father found work as a farm laborer and cannery employee. Chet Cunningham remembered eating lots of oatmeal and grapefruit because both were cheap.

At Pacific University in Forest Grove, he failed an English entrance exam. A professor warned him that he might not make it as a journalist. Cunningham was stung, but he managed to sell a few magazine stories and earn a journalism degree. Drafted into the Army, he was sent into combat during the Korean War. Then he attended Columbia University in New York, where he received a master's in journalism in 1954.

He worked for small newspapers and wrote training materials. In his free time, he wrote a novel about his war experiences. He couldn't sell it. After more rejections, he decided to try Westerns. He was told publishers paid less for them than for other types of novels, so he figured there would be less competition. His Westerns—with titles like *Apache Ambush* and *Ride Tall, Hang High*—became his family's bread and butter.

Cunningham created a group of San Diego–based writers who met regularly to critique one another's work and share ideas. His advice to novice writers was simple: "Put your butt in the chair and do it." That, of course, applies to anyone who might want to write a life story.

RICHARD JENRETTE (1929–2018), the co-founder of a Wall Street securities firm, should be remembered for being true to his own quirky habits. He was an untraditional boss who quizzed job candidates about their astrological signs and favorite colors and sought psychological clues in their penmanship. In his free time, he indulged a love of tradition by acquiring 19th-century mansions on impulse and hiring decorators to adorn them with antiques and leather-bound books bought in bulk.

Each morning he weighed himself before breakfast, then plotted the result on graph paper so he could take immediate action, such as skipping bread at lunch, if he veered off target. Instead of going to a gym, he started his days at home with 50 push-ups, 50 deep knee bends, and a burst of running in place.

He believed in making a well-conceived plan and then ignoring the critics. He often quoted a proverb: "The dog barks but the caravan moves on."

Born in Raleigh, North Carolina, he was the son of an insurance agent. As a boy he liked drawing houses. He found his family's Tudor-style home lacking in architectural distinction. Already, he was aiming higher.

At the University of North Carolina, he majored in journalism and was editor of the student newspaper. He worked as a sportswriter and a life insurance agent in his teens and early 20s before concluding those were not likely paths to wealth. So he made a long-term investment in himself by enrolling at Harvard Business School, where he graduated in 1957.

The Harvard degree earned him a job at Brown Brothers Harriman, a venerable Wall Street firm where he admired the oak-paneled walls, fireplaces, and rolltop desks. He started as a messenger, toting bags of securities, before learning to write research reports. After mastering basic research, he was allowed to manage the money of wealthy clients. One of them was Greta Garbo.

Before he got a chance to meet the reclusive actress in person, however, a more tempting proposition emerged. William Donaldson and Dan Lufkin, fellow Harvard Business School graduates, persuaded him to join them as a partner in a new firm.

Starting a new firm, he thought, was smarter than waiting two decades in the hope of becoming a partner at Brown Brothers. So, in 1959, he teamed up with his friends in launching Donaldson, Lufkin & Jenrette, or DLJ. He decorated the new firm's office with antiques and oil paintings to suggest an illustrious history, one way to reassure clients.

In the go-go 1960s, DLJ flourished as a research house, trader, and fund manager. In 1974, when Jenrette became CEO, everything started to go wrong. Oil prices and interest rates soared. Stock prices and trading volumes sank. Wall Street firms braced for the end of fixed stock-trading commissions, opening the way for freer competition, which would slash their incomes.

Lufkin favored turning DLJ into a smaller, more specialized investment firm. Jenrette insisted on keeping DLJ mostly intact, partly because he didn't want to lay off colleagues in troubled times.

The dogs barked, and the caravan rumbled on. DLJ survived.

When he couldn't sleep at night, Jenrette listed his worries on a yellow legal pad he kept at his bedside, according to his 1997 memoir, *The Contrarian Manager*. He saved those lists of worries and crossed them out one by one as they were resolved. It was his way of shedding negative thoughts.

IN 2017, I decided to write an obituary about J. Dewey Daane (1918–2017) mainly because of a single incident that, I felt, illuminated his character.

Daane had an impressive résumé: He had earned a doctorate in public administration at Harvard University, advised Paraguay on financial matters, and served on the U.S. Federal Reserve Board of Governors from 1963 to 1974. A good résumé doesn't necessarily make for a memorable story, however.

To me, Daane's finest moment came in 1966, when he visited Spain for an American Bankers Association conference. He and other bankers took a break from that conference to visit a bullring near Toledo.

The day's event was a *tienta*, or trial, rather than a bullfight. Even so, the animals were fearsome, according to a *Wall Street Journal* account: "A small tornado of dust emerges, followed a few seconds later by a black thunderbolt of muscle and horns."

The organizers of this trial sought volunteers to wave a cape in front of one of the animals. "Somebody's got to do it!" Daane announced, according to his widow, Barbara McMann Daane. "The next thing I knew," she said, "Dewey was down in the ring."

The 47-year-old Federal Reserve governor, dapper in sunglasses and a business suit, flicked a scarlet-and-yellow cape. Within seconds, he was "draped over the neck of the still-galloping beast," the *Journal* reported. "After [what seemed like] an eternity, Dewey Daane slides off the animal and lands firmly upright."

Daane escaped with mere bruises. As a souvenir, he kept a stuffed bull's head on his office wall at the Federal Reserve.

Close observers of the Fed would not have been entirely surprised by Daane's derring-do in Spain: In December 1965, he cast the deciding vote for an interest-rate increase opposed vigorously by President Lyndon B. Johnson.

Few of us will ever defy a president or have a fling in a bullring. Nearly all of us have faced moments when we had to decide whether to play it safe or have an adventure. Make sure to include those in your story.

# CHAPTER 16

# *The Wandering Armenian*

Vartan Gregorian (1934–2021) is remembered for saving the New York Public Library. He should also be known for preserving his own remarkable story.

Gregorian dubbed himself the "wandering Armenian." After immigrating to the United States in his early 20s with barely enough money to buy lunch, he earned a PhD in history at Stanford, taught at UCLA and the University of Texas, was provost at the University of Pennsylvania, rescued the New York Public Library from squalor in the 1980s, served as president of Brown University, and finally headed the Carnegie Foundation in New York, where his office featured the portrait of another striving immigrant, Andrew Carnegie.

He was so busy researching and explaining the history of the world that he never had much time to think about his personal history. Then, when he was in his mid-60s, Gregorian found himself confined to a hospital bed for an extended spell while he was, as he put it, "separated from my left kidney."

Having had time to ponder how much longer he might live, Gregorian started outlining a memoir. "I decided to write the book," he told an NPR interviewer in 2003, "because my three sons and many of my friends only knew public Gregorian, public persona, but not the private one."

It wasn't vanity or a fear that his name would be forgotten. It was already engraved on the scores of honorary degrees and other awards he had collected. His children and friends already knew about his triumphs. His real motive for writing, he said, was that he felt an obligation to tell them about his mistakes and struggles, "so they would not think that everything in one's life has been just serendipity."

Gregorian's story—told in his 2003 memoir, *The Road to Home*—begins in Tabriz, a town in northwestern Iran, where he was born into an Armenian family in 1934. Once a stop on the Silk Road trading route between East and West, Tabriz was a place of pleasant summers and gardens, as well as harsh winters, and "minor and major earthquakes and devastating plagues, including typhus and cholera, not to mention smallpox," he wrote.

His paternal grandfather owned a caravansary, which Gregorian described as "a sort of animal parking lot." His father, an accountant, worked as a middle manager at an oil company.

America was a faraway paradise defined by movies he saw. It was, he surmised as a schoolboy, a very clean country and therefore must be lacking in ants. If there were no ants, he wondered, what could zoos feed to their anteaters? That thought led to a short-lived enterprise in which he and his younger sister killed thousands of black ants so they could be exported to America. The project ended abruptly when a second-grade teacher assured him that America had plenty of ants.

His father spoke English but never sought to teach it to his son and showed little interest in his children's education in general. His mother died young, leaving the young Vartan and his sister in the care of their maternal grandmother, an illiterate peasant who put a high priority on education and enriched his mind with fables and proverbs that he remembered for the rest of his life:

"Good advice, like good medicine, is hard to swallow."
"The stomach is an oven. If there is adequate fuel in it,
    don't overburden it."
"Don't insult a crocodile before you cross a river."

YOURS TRULY — 117

In his childhood home he found only two books, a Bible and a world history textbook. At the age of 11, he became a part-time assistant at a library, a job that put literature into his eager grasp. One of his early favorite books was Victor Hugo's *Les Misérables*.

A leader in the Armenian community noted the boy's intelligence and helped him move to Beirut at age 15 to study at an Armenian college. "I read ferociously," he recalled. Though he had so little money that he sometimes went hungry, the local Armenian community sustained him. To survive in school, he learned French and began to master English.

Support from his teachers and benefactors helped him win admission to Stanford University. Newly arrived in the United States in 1956, he saved money by dining on soup, liver and tea at a Chinese restaurant.

While preparing to begin his classes at Stanford, he feared that the many distractions of the San Francisco Bay Area would divert him from his studies. This anxiety led to what he called "one of the most stupid deeds of my life." The way to avoid the temptations of social life, he decided, was to shave his head. He didn't realize that he should have cut his hair down to a stubble before attempting to shave off the rest. Instead, he simply lathered up his hair with shaving cream and began shaving.

By the time he was finished, his scalp was a disaster area of gouges, and he was struggling to stop the bleeding. Recalling a remedy used by religious zealots who flagellated themselves, he applied egg yolks to his wounds and finally found some relief. For weeks afterward, he covered up his wounds with a beret.

Gregorian also confesses his misadventures in love, including exchanges of passionate letters with a young woman in Iran who turned out to have a fiancé. Later, he and some other foreign students were shocked to find that young American women might kiss and snuggle them without being in love.

One day at Stanford he spotted "a tall, blond young woman who was playing an entrancing Joplin ragtime on the piano." She was Clare Russell, a history major from Tenafly, New Jersey, whose ancestors had arrived in America on the *Mayflower*. "She had utter self-confidence, great poise and an elegant walk," he wrote in his memoir. They married in 1960.

Gregorian wrote a history of Afghanistan and began teaching at San Francisco State College while completing his PhD at Stanford. By his mid-30s, he was a full professor at the University of Texas in Austin. Something about his charisma and enthusiasm made people see him as a leader. The University of Pennsylvania recruited him as a history professor and soon promoted him to dean of arts and sciences and then provost.

By 1980, he was a leading candidate to become Penn's president. One of his detractors on the board of trustees suggested that Gregorian, with his foreign accent and manners, might be too uncivilized for the job. In the end, the trustees passed over him to choose an outsider. Gregorian got the news from a radio news report.

"I could cope with rejection but not insult and humiliation," he wrote later. He resigned as provost and was soon offered an alternative that came out of left field: the presidency of the New York Public Library.

The attractions of the job were not immediately obvious. New York's near-bankruptcy in the 1970s had starved the library and other public institutions of resources. The library's central building, a Beaux-Arts monument, was crumbling. Its 88 miles of bookshelves hadn't been dusted in 75 years. Drug dealers and pimps congregated on its peripheries. The back of the building, facing Bryant Park, had become, as Gregorian put it, "New York's longest urinal."

Yet when Gregorian saw the trustees' faith in his ability to save the library, he decided to take on the challenge. He applied his charm and exuberance to persuade the mayor, city council, and New York society squires that the library could and must be saved. Libraries and museums, he declared, were "the only institutions that granted and preserved immortality on earth."

With help from new friends including Brooke Astor and David Rockefeller, he raised $327 million from public and private sources. He discovered that New Yorkers would compete to pay large sums for the honor of sitting next to famous authors at library events. That helped pay for humidity controls to protect books, scrubbing of blackened facades, and restoration of elegant rooms that had been chopped into cubicles.

Gregorian relished life in the city. "New York was full of chutzpah," he wrote, "and I was full of chutzpah." He joyfully cultivated local politicians, philanthropists, and business leaders. His schedule of lunches, dinners, and cocktail parties was so full that he gained nearly 40 pounds. While renovating the main library, which he called "the People's Palace," he also improved facilities and services at more than 80 branches scattered around the city.

After eight exhausting years of running the library, Gregorian began to miss academia and even, he said, academic politics. He accepted a call from Brown University and served as president there from 1989 to 1997. He then headed the Carnegie Corporation of New York for more than two decades. He was finally giving away money rather than begging for it.

One of his sons, Vahe Gregorian, a sports columnist for the *Kansas City Star*, recalled his father's dogged efforts to understand and appreciate American sports. At baseball games, he would ask why there was no longstop to go with the shortstop. After the Kansas City Chiefs lost the 2021 Super Bowl to Tampa Bay, the father sent his son this analysis: "They need more fat guys."

Gregorian died in April 2021 at the age of 87. He had led a life no one could have imagined.

In a 2005 commencement address at the University of Notre Dame, he left students with this thought: "Much of life is about the routine, not the extraordinary, but do not let the routine distract you from your pursuit of the exceptional."

Gregorian was exceptional in many ways, not least for the way he made time to tell his story so vividly. Even for those of us with less dramatic lives, his memoir is a model of storytelling.

# CHAPTER 17

# *Being Frank About the Family*

Obituaries—typically stuffed with references to adoring spouses and beloved children—rarely acknowledge even the slightest friction within the family.

That is one reason I wanted to write about George H. Walker III (1931–2020), a cousin of President George H.W. Bush.

Walker had plenty of accomplishments to decorate his curriculum vitae and fill an impressive obituary. A graduate of Yale University and Harvard Law School, he went on to head a St. Louis–based investment bank and serve as U.S. ambassador to Hungary. His pedigree ensured all the introductions he would ever need.

Yet there was much more to his story than the public or even many of his friends could know. As I learned in doing research to write his obituary, it wasn't always easy being George H. Walker III.

He made what I consider a wise choice: telling his side of the story. After reading excerpts from the family history he prepared and talking with people who knew him, I concluded that he spent the first half of his life striving to please his father and the second half charting his own course.

The second act was far more successful.

George Herbert Walker III, known as Bert, was born March 16, 1931, in St. Louis and grew up in Greenwich, Connecticut. He was the firstborn son. The expectations of his father, George Herbert "Herbie" Walker Jr., were high enough to induce acrophobia.

Herbie, Bert's dad, took baseball seriously. He had played on the Yale team; he later helped found the New York Mets. Herbie sent Bert to the elite Groton boarding school, where the young man tried out as a catcher on the baseball team but developed a mysterious inability to throw the ball accurately, apparently because of a mental block. He ended up on the bench. His father, watching from the stands, transferred his hopes to Bert's younger brother, Ray, a star shortstop.

The father was a Yale man, so there was no need to wonder where Bert Walker was headed. He enrolled at Yale in 1949. Among his biggest anxieties was whether he would earn admission to the Skull and Bones secret society, in line with his father's expectation. This time he was able to gratify the old man.

After graduating from Yale in 1953, he enrolled at Harvard Law School. Dean Acheson, the former U.S. Secretary of State, had once mentioned to Bert Walker's father that Harvard Law School had trained his mind. That impressed father and son.

After two years in the Air Force, doing legal chores at the Wright-Patterson base in Ohio, Bert Walker went to work for his father at G.H. Walker & Co., the family-owned securities firm. He worked as a securities salesman in St. Louis and then built up a profitable branch of the firm in Chicago.

"We all saw Bert as the one who should succeed his father," said Jonathan Bush, a cousin who also worked at G.H. Walker. When it came time to appoint a new president in 1971, however, Bert's dad chose Fred Wonham.

One of his father's housekeepers explained the situation bluntly to Bert: "You're the last person your dad would ever pick to run that firm."

The family sold G.H. Walker & Co. to White, Weld & Co. in 1974. Seeing little future for himself at White, Weld, Bert sought opportunities elsewhere. George Newton, a former G.H. Walker banker who had become chairman of Stifel, Nicolaus & Co., in St. Louis, hired

Bert as an executive vice president. Four years later he became CEO, a job he held successfully until 1992.

Bert founded an institute at Eden Theological Seminary in St. Louis to teach business leaders how to deal with moral and ethical issues, while infusing church leaders with business and financial skills.

In his later years, he did a three-minute plank exercise each morning, propping himself up on his elbows and toes while singing the hymn "Abide With Me," reciting the Lord's Prayer, and praying for loved ones. He regularly rode his three-wheel bike for breakfast or lunch in Kennebunkport, Maine, his summer home. His usual lunch order was half an egg-salad sandwich and a glass of chocolate milk. Though he ordered only half a sandwich, he insisted on paying for a whole one.

Bert Walker took charge of his narrative. He wasn't the rich kid who could never please his dad. He was the one who took a while to find his own niche, and then made the most of it.

ANTHONY DOWNS (1930–2021) had no such early traumas. Born in Chicago, he was co-valedictorian of his high school in suburban Park Ridge, Illinois, and proceeded to Carleton College in Northfield, Minnesota. Making use of his gift for debate and public speaking, Downs ran for student body president at Carleton. One opponent called him a "silver-tongued son of a bitch," but Downs won the election by a large margin.

Though he delivered on all of his campaign promises, Downs noticed that Carleton students paid little or no attention to his efforts on their behalf. That was rational, he concluded, because his actions as student president "were mostly irrelevant to their lives."

Downs won a scholarship for graduate school at Stanford, where he studied economics. His mentors included Kenneth J. Arrow, later the winner of a Nobel Prize in economics. While considering ideas for his doctoral thesis, Downs thought back to his experience in Carleton College politics. He applied economic methods to create a theoretical model explaining the motivations of voters and political candidates.

Downs posited that American voters and politicians, no matter how lazy or lunatic they may appear at times, tend to behave rationally. Most voters, knowing that a single vote almost never swings an election, devote little time to trying to figure out which candidate's positions make the most sense. He called their behavior "rational ignorance." Politicians, in turn, rationally gravitate toward centrist positions in two-party races to attract the largest number of voters.

His thesis was published in 1957 as a book, *An Economic Theory of Democracy*. More than six decades later, when Downs died, his name was still familiar among political scientists.

Over his career, Downs wrote two dozen books on topics including traffic jams (we will never eliminate them, he concluded), racial strife, housing for the poor, and bureaucracy. None of those books came close to matching the sales of his magnificent doctoral thesis.

Around age 80, at the urging of some of his five children, Downs sat down to write something he knew would never reach a wide audience: his life story. He called it *The Life and Times of Anthony Downs*. It filled 157 pages. Never intended for publication, it was a gift to his family.

Along with his triumphs, Downs includes embarrassments. In a description of an otherwise idyllic tour of the Rocky Mountains and western Canada with his sisters during his graduate school years, he confesses that they accused him of not showering frequently enough.

He recalls family road trips in a green Buick station wagon. While he extolled the scenery, the children squirmed and sulked in the back seat. "They always wanted to get something to eat or go to the bathroom or arrive at our next camping ground." In one of his Christmas letters, he reported that he had been traveling with "a beautiful girl [his wife] and five idiots."

When the family transferred from the Chicago suburbs to McLean, Virginia, he arrived early to start work at the Brookings Institution, leaving his wife to manage the move of five children and a large dog on her own. "I greatly regret leaving that difficult task to Kay and the kids," he writes.

In his life story, Downs mentions his disappointment over certain behavior of some of his children when they were teenagers or young adults. He describes his own humiliation late in his career when colleagues told him that his latest study of democracy wasn't up to par.

Providing what many would consider too much information, he writes graphically about late-in-life health problems. "Sorry to mention all these gory details," he adds, "but my children asked me to leave them all in!"

No doubt his children cringed at a few passages when they read this life story. They might have quibbled with some of the details. Yet I suspect they were grateful to have their dad's unvarnished version of what his life was all about, along with his affirmations of love for them.

> When you write a life story, you don't have to give away all your secrets or resurrect all your family feuds.

WHEN YOU WRITE a life story, you don't have to give away all your secrets or resurrect all your family feuds. It helps, however, to own up to at least some of your shortcomings, acknowledge the occasional clash with relatives, and admit that things didn't always go as you had planned.

# CHAPTER 18

# *What? Nothing Much Happened?*

Iris Westman grew up in rural North Dakota. She taught in public schools, worked as a librarian, never lived very far from her birthplace, and never married or had children. It all sounds pretty uneventful. How much could I hope to say about her life?

Well, for one thing, she lived to be 115 years old.

She died in January 2021 at a nursing home in Northwood, North Dakota. She had been listed by the Gerontology Research Group as the second-oldest living American.

By chance, I met Iris in 2016 and spent an hour asking her about her long life. I was struck by her serenity. Maybe, I thought, it had something to do with what she didn't do—watch television news or engage with social media. Maybe it also had to do with her rare ability to be content with what she had.

At the time we met, Donald Trump was campaigning for president and stirring up all kinds of passions across America. "I've heard of him," Iris said. "Not enough to express an opinion."

She had more to say about Warren G. Harding, who served as president from 1921 until his death in 1923. Harding may not have been a great president, Iris said, but she remembered having a soft spot for him: "He was awfully good looking."

Iris could no longer see well enough to read easily but enjoyed listening to audiobooks. History and travel were her preferred themes.

Her nursing home offered daily gatherings for cards, bingo, or other amusements. Though she sometimes took part in those activities, she said, "I don't need to have lots of things going on. I can be quite content sitting here and looking out the window and not seeing anything." Outside, the Red River Valley was flat and drifted with snow.

During the interview, she sat upright and poised in a plush easy chair. Her hair was stylishly waved. She wore a knit top with a geometrical pattern over wine-colored slacks. Near her chair was a folder containing a letter the White House sent her in 2015 to congratulate her on her 110th birthday.

She offered no secrets to longevity. "You just sit back and it happens," she said. "The Lord takes care of it, and He knows what He's doing, so we should just sit back and let Him do it."

Born on August 28, 1905, she grew up on a farm near Aneta, North Dakota, with her parents and three brothers. Her parents, of Norwegian descent, encouraged their children to read at an early age. When she got to first grade, Iris was shocked to find that some of her fellow students hadn't yet begun reading. "I thought, For pity's sakes!" she recalled.

The family had a Ford car but needed horse-drawn sleds to get around in the winter because roads often vanished beneath the snow. She remembered the pleasing scent of candles burning on the Christmas tree during a brief home service each December. One of her brothers would stand by with a pail of water in case of fire. Presents were few: "We'd get one fun gift, like a toy, and otherwise we'd get something new to wear."

After graduating from the University of North Dakota in 1928, she taught English at several schools in North Dakota and Minnesota. Later she studied library science and became the librarian at an elementary school, until retiring in 1972. She preferred working with younger children. "Teenagers were getting to be a little difficult to deal with, and I didn't want to fight them, so I stayed with the elementary school," she said. "Which means I'm a coward."

I asked Iris whether she had ever come close to getting married. "Well, a couple of times, but I think it was very well that I didn't."

She fondly remembered a kitten once given to her by a neighbor. It was so scruffy and unsightly at first sight that she mockingly named it Aphrodite, after the Greek goddess, only to realize later it was a male cat. "He was a very smart cat," she said.

Other favorite memories included travels to the East Coast, a cruise through the Great Lakes, and tours of Scandinavia and Western Europe.

As for politics, she was willing to assume almost any crisis could be survived. When Franklin Roosevelt died, she said, "I thought, Oh, what's going to happen to the country? I figured what did Truman know? But he stepped up and was very good."

If you were summing up Iris's life, you might be tempted to say nothing much happened. Yet her story was one of the most popular obituaries I ever wrote.

I WROTE ABOUT another woman whose face was briefly in the public eye, though her name never was. Carmen Collins (1952–2021), raised on Chicago's South Side, noticed in the late 1960s that Black women like her were starting to show up as models in mainstream publications. It seemed like an opportunity.

She found an agent and for a few years was featured in ads for Greyhound Lines and other companies. She was in clothing ads and catalogs. Sometimes she earned more than $100 an hour, but she never hit the big time. After the failure of an early marriage, she found herself the single mother of three boys.

She wanted to get them into better schools and away from gangs. So, even though it meant losing some of her support system of inner-city friends and relatives, she moved the family to the western suburbs of Chicago, where she reinvented herself as a real estate broker.

At the new school, some of the white kids threw snowballs and ice chunks at her sons. They came home bruised. She gave them a pep talk about sticking up for themselves.

To supplement her income, Carmen bought merchandise in bulk—fishing poles, say, or beauty products—and sold it at flea markets or online. "My mother was the first dollar store," one of her sons said.

She often told her sons they needed PMA, short for a positive mental attitude. Then she would smile and add, "Know what I mean, Jelly Bean?"

> If you think your life has been uneventful, think again. Once you start writing, you may find it's been far more interesting than you realized.

THOUGH FEW SUSPECTED it, Iris and Carmen had surprising and inspiring stories to tell. If you think your life has been uneventful, think again. Once you start writing, you may find it's been far more interesting than you realized.

Know what I mean, Jelly Bean?

# CHAPTER 19

# *How We Failed My Father*

I N THE SPRING OF 1997, the Red River flooded far more copiously than usual and destroyed large sections of my hometown, Grand Forks, North Dakota. During the flood, a fire broke out and incinerated several buildings downtown. The banner headline in the local newspaper the next morning read, "Come Hell and High Water." The situation was so dangerous that the U.S. Coast Guard made what may have been its first appearance in landlocked North Dakota (1,500 miles from the nearest ocean) to help ferry people to safety.

For the first time, floodwater reached my parents' neighborhood and filled their basement. With thousands of others, they had to flee. In the middle of the night they drove to Bismarck, North Dakota, where my sister Gail lives.

My father had suffered strokes and had kidney cancer, among other ailments. The flood was a further upset to his equilibrium. From my apartment in Hong Kong, I called the hospital where he was being treated and asked to be connected to his room. After a delay, a hospital worker returned to the line to say my father was dead. My mother had not yet been able to reach me with the news.

Among the dozens of other urgent tasks occasioned by his death, we had to prepare an obituary for the local papers. You might think we were in a good position to do that. My father had been a journalist for his entire adult life and could have written, years earlier, at least a brief summary of his life. He didn't. If he ever even thought of it, I'm sure he didn't see that task as a priority. My mother and I were both full-time journalists, and my sisters, despite being lawyers, knew very well how to write in plain English. Yet we were totally unprepared.

My defense: At that time, my job had nothing to do with obituaries. I had never given any thought to how they should be written or why they mattered.

My mom, who had just lost her husband after 48 years of marriage and had many other things to worry about, needed to write his story quickly. She did it adequately but without her usual flair.

Here is what she wrote:

Jack Hagerty, 78, retired editor of the *Grand Forks Herald*, died June 13, 1997, in the Mandan [N.D.] hospital.

Jack Hagerty was born Dec. 14, 1918, in Aberdeen, S.D., near the family home at Monango. He grew up in Aberdeen and got his start in the newspaper business as a student working for the *American-News*. He attended Northern State Teachers College before transferring to South Dakota State College at Brookings, S.D., where he graduated in 1940. He was editor of the college newspaper, the *Collegian*. He spent one summer as acting editor of the Lemmon, S.D., *Leader*.

He was a veteran of World War II, when he served on a U.S. Navy coding board in Brazil. Following the war, he worked briefly for the *Aberdeen American-News* and for the *Daily Sentinel* at Grand Junction, Colo. He returned to this area as a correspondent for United Press in Bismarck in 1946. In 1953, he became Minnesota manager for United Press and was based in Minneapolis before going to Grand Forks in 1957 as news editor of the

*Herald.* He also served as managing editor before he was named editor. He retired in 1983. During his years with the *Herald*, the newspaper won two national awards from the Associated Press.

He was chairman of the News Executives Conference of the University of Minnesota; president of the North Dakota Associated Press; president of the North Dakota Chapter of Sigma Delta Chi, the Society of Professional Journalists; and chaired the North Dakota Fair Trial–Free Press Commission and the UND Journalism Advisory Committee.

In 1985, he was honored by the North Dakota Newspaper Association for 50 years in the newspaper business. He was honored in April as a distinguished alumnus from the communications department at South Dakota State College.

He also wrote a biography of the founder of the *Grand Forks Herald* as one of the North Dakota Mini-Biography Series for the North Dakota Heritage Center. It is entitled, *The Reformer: George B. Winship.*

Many readers would see nothing wrong with this obituary. It gave an accurate summary of my father's life, listed his survivors, and mentioned awards and honors.

To me, in retrospect, it was a failure. We conveyed nothing of my father's personality. We were silent on what he was trying to do with his life and why. We preserved no examples of his quirks and sense of humor. We blew it.

Even if I had tried to write his story, I would have struggled. I lived in my father's house for my first 18 years and saw him at least once a year for the next 20-some. How can it be that I knew so little about him?

Even the basic facts are blurry. Here is what little I know:

He grew up in Aberdeen, South Dakota. His father's family—of Irish, English, Scottish, and Norwegian descent—had made money in real estate, and then lost it in the Great Depression. For reasons unknown to me, the family at one point lit out for Washington State and then a few years later returned to South Dakota. I never got a clear answer about how my grandfather passed his time—only an impression that whatever he did amounted to little. To save money during the Depression, my grandmother sewed underwear for her children out of old flour sacks. The family dog was named Rex.

My father's older brother, darkly handsome and charming, joined the Air Force and died in an airplane crash during World War II. My father spent the war as a decoder of messages for the Navy, in the safety of Rio de Janeiro. He had an English girlfriend there. Much later, my mother, having seen a picture of the English girl leaning against a palm tree, declared that her legs were fat. Jealousy, like love, can be retroactive.

He came back with a white sharkskin suit, soon to be stowed in the back of a closet, and a deep tan, never completely lost. My mom said he looked like a Brazil nut. I suspect that nothing in the rest of his life lived up to being a young man at liberty to prowl the beaches and lounges of Rio.

Once the war and the tropical adventures were over, he returned to his native region and became a journalist. He wrote tersely about politics, floods, droughts, and crimes. Eventually he became the editor of a newspaper and had a sufficient income to raise his family in upper-middle-class comfort and to buy a new Oldsmobile every five years. The stolid Oldsmobile was his chosen stratum, clearly superior to the common Chevrolet, yet below the ostentatious Cadillac. If he ever yearned for something sportier, we didn't know about it.

He was an old-style newspaperman, right out of a 1940s movie. Cigarette clenched on one side of his mouth, typing with two fingers. When he interviewed people, he didn't take notes. He remembered everything. Or so he said.

On Wednesday evenings, boys' night out, he played cribbage with a few friends at the country club. My mother, my sisters, and I exploited his absence those nights by eating pizza, a dish he disdained. He also played golf—doggedly, badly, and as far as I could tell, without much enjoyment. Walking around a nine-hole course was what he called exercise. I never knew him to pursue any other form of physical exertion. Nor did he concern himself with nutrition or personal appearance. He had new clothing only when my mother bought it and seemed perfectly indifferent to his attire so long as it consisted of a suit, white shirt, and necktie.

On domestic matters—vacations, child discipline, home furnishings, social life—he deferred entirely to my mother. In the evening, if she felt inclined to lean against the kitchen counter, with a drink in her hand, and recount the frustrations of her day, he listened with no sign of impatience and with all of the desired signals of polite commiseration. He rarely, if ever, contributed his own lamentations.

My mother recalls him as a good father, willing to plop down on the carpeting at the end of a workday to play with his toddlers. I remember him as an excellent reader of bedtime stories, including *Winnie the Pooh*. My sisters and I delighted in his pronunciation of "Eeyore"—with an extended, high-pitched stress on the first syllable. We asked him to repeat it over and over, and he always obliged.

In the summer, after work, he was willing to play catch with me, tossing a baseball back and forth across our backyard. Although I didn't suspect it at the time, I now realize that playing catch probably was no great amusement for him. He also took me to baseball games and taught me the notations used to keep track of each ball, strike, hit, and out on a scorecard.

We both cherished the lore of long-dead baseball players like Enos Slaughter or Pie Traynor. To pass the time on long car trips, we played a game in which one of us would say the last name of a major league baseball player, current or past, and the other would have to respond with the name of another player whose last name started with the final letter in the name of the preceding player. So if I said Musial, my dad could say Lemon, and I could follow up with Niekro, leading to Oliva or Ott. We could carry this on for hours.

At some point, my mother and father made a vow to give up smoking. Both would quit at once and for all time. My mother kept her side of the bargain. My father pretended to keep his. We were always amazed that he went to work, at least for an hour or so, every day of the year. Even Christmas. Only much later did I figure out that part of his mission was to get out of the house and enjoy a cigarette.

Once I brought a girlfriend home. Afterwards she commented, "You and your father don't talk!" Oh, we did talk a little, but only of baseball or other safe subjects. Never of politics or anything very personal or upsetting. He was retired by then. He liked to watch a quiz show on TV and read Dick Francis novels. Every evening, at exactly five, he poured himself the first of exactly two drinks.

The last time I spoke to him was over a phone line connecting Hong Kong to North Dakota. So weak that he could barely talk, he nonetheless wanted to say something about his favorite baseball team, the Chicago White Sox. When he tried to say the name of a star player, Albert Belle, he could utter only the first two syllables: "Al-ber..." Those choked syllables were the last he spoke to me.

A few months later I saw my father in a dream. We were walking down a wooded path and—unaccountably, uncharacteristically—we joined hands. His hand felt large and pillowy on my boy's hand. We both realized at the same instant that we were saying goodbye forever. With perfect synchronization, tears spilled from our eyes.

DAD, YOU MAY not have been very flashy, but you did a good job after all. I appreciate it more now than I could have then. Not to quibble, but I do wish you had told us your story. I bet it would have surprised us. I'm sure we would have read every word and kept it in a safe place.

WHILE I'M IN confessional mode, I should acknowledge that I also failed to do justice to my sister Carol when she died of amyotrophic lateral sclerosis, known as ALS or Lou Gehrig's disease, in December 2011, at the age of 56.

Two days before she died, Carol asked me to write her obituary.

There was a lot to say about Carol. She had bummed around Europe, waited on tables, gone to law school, and worked as a lawyer in Washington, Hong Kong, Tokyo, New York, and Denver. Then she met a handsome rancher named Curt Werner in northeastern Colorado. In an outdoor ceremony on the banks of the South Platte River, with guests seated on hay bales, they got married. They had three children.

When Carol died, I was not yet an obituary writer. In haste, without a clue about how to proceed, I gathered the basic facts of her existence. Because Carol could barely speak at that point, I had to consult LinkedIn to get the details on her university degrees and employers. I ended up with an accurate but dull recitation of degrees, jobs, and family connections. The real Carol, her unique personality, was missing.

I tried to compensate by writing a eulogy. A few excerpts:

> Where others saw hurdles and difficulties, Carol saw opportunities and adventures.
>
> When she was little, if you told her something was too hard, that made her more determined to do it. Other little girls baked cookies. Carol made baked Alaska—and even though it turned into a gooey mess, it was a sort of triumph.
>
> It was a dog that led her to Merino, Colorado. Or rather, two dogs—Bill and Daffy.
>
> They were Gordon setters. After Carol bought them in Denver, she figured out that they were hunting dogs, not city dogs.
>
> Though she had never before picked up a gun or been anywhere near a duck blind, Carol decided she owed it to her dogs to learn to hunt with them. On one of her first ventures into the exotic world of duck hunting, she met Curt. The choice of a dog can be surprisingly consequential.
>
> Carol moved to the ranch and decorated it in a strange blend of artifacts from New York, Tokyo, and Washington County, Colorado. Somehow, that blend worked. She cooked elaborate meals on her immense Viking range.

Even her diagnosis with ALS struck Carol as a sort of adventure. She would find a way to live with the disease as well as she could, as long as she could. She would take part in pharmaceutical trials. She learned to zip around in a motorized wheelchair, scattering dachshunds in her wake. She learned to operate a computer by clicking her eyelids. In our last game of Scrabble, she won.

The disease progressed faster than anyone expected. Soon Carol was almost totally paralyzed. Friends streamed in from all over the world to comfort her.

Her cousin Kris Hartley drove in weekly from Colorado Springs, bearing meals and loving care. "She's the best tooth brusher you could ask for," Carol said of Kris.

Carol always had faith in technology and scientific progress. She was the first to adopt any new electronic device. She believed in biofuels, even after she poured an experimental variety into her Saab and destroyed the engine.

In the end, technology let her down. Computer software and pharmaceuticals were no match for the relentless attack of ALS.

Carol's sense of humor and her faith in her family, friends, and God never let her down. In her final hours, she was serene. She made little jokes. She was ready, as she put it, to be free of her broken body and embrace eternal life.

"Be good," she told us. "I'll be watching."

# CHAPTER 20

# *How I Wrote My Mother's Amazing Story*

I FIRST WROTE MY MOM'S life story in 2004. She was 78 years old. It seemed like a good time to put her tale into writing. At that age, I figured, how much more could happen to her?

Way more than I could have imagined.

As a professional journalist, my mom, Marilyn Hagerty, could have written her own story, of course. I knew she probably wouldn't. So I arranged to sit down with her for several hours. I asked questions. She answered. I scribbled notes.

When it came time to write, I had to figure out where to begin. Despite my general preference for chronological order, I decided to start with an incident from my mom's early days as a reporter. It was the kind of episode that would define her working life:

After graduating from the University of South Dakota, Marilyn worked as a reporter for the *American News* in Aberdeen, South Dakota, known as the Hub City. Editors there wanted her to write for the society section, covering weddings, women's clubs, and the like. "I told them I didn't go to college to work in the society department," she said. So she was assigned to write feature stories as well as covering the hospital and the school board.

One evening in 1949, after a rainstorm, she slipped while trying to cross a street and fell into a trench, dug for a construction project and now swirling with muddy water. In one hand, she was clutching a letter to her fiancé; in the other, a bag of Hershey's chocolates.

She flailed in the frigid water and groped for something solid to grasp. Finally, she reached the far side of the trench and managed to pull herself out. Her new raincoat was soaked and smeared with clay. Two policemen guided her to their squad car and put her in the back seat, next to a stray dog.

They drove her to her boarding house on Kline Street. Her landlady, Mrs. Bosman, spread out newspapers inside the door. Marilyn peeled off her sopping clothes.

She was still clutching the Hershey's chocolates.

The story soon spread around the *American News* office. The publisher of the paper, Henry Schmidt, suggested that Marilyn should write "one of her funny stories" about her adventure.

It was a busy day for news. The Chinese Communists were invading Shanghai. Tornadoes and floods had killed 14 people in Texas and Oklahoma. Yet the next morning those stories were overshadowed by Marilyn's account of her fall. The page one headline read: "Only a Swimmer's Safe on Hub Streets!"

She concluded her story with a description of her return to the street where she slipped:

> A trip back to the scene of the swim somewhat soothed my damaged pride.
> The ditch was actually almost 10 feet wide and 8 feet deep in the center.
> Workmen erecting a boardwalk and fences explained to me that "some girl came along here and fell in last night."
> "Yes," I said, "I know."

AFTER THAT INTRODUCTION, it was time for me to revert to chronological order:

Marilyn Gail Hansen was born May 30, 1926, in Pierre, South Dakota. Her father, Mads Hansen, known to American friends as Matt, grew up in the village of Kolby Kas on the small green island of Samso in Denmark, where his family lived in a house with a thatched roof and adjoining barn. He was the sixth of nine children. Because the farm was too small to be divided among so many brothers and sisters, Mads emigrated to the U.S. at age 22. After an 11-day voyage on the ship *Oscar II*, he landed in New York in June 1908.

Mads was six foot one and lean. He walked with a limp because a bone he had broken as a boy never healed properly. He tried his hand as a farmer in Haakon County, South Dakota, under the Homestead Act, which provided free land in desolate parts of the Great Plains for those willing to cultivate. The land was poor, and farming didn't work out for him. He drifted to Pierre and found work as a shipping clerk at a wholesale grocery company. He and his friends drank their own home-brewed beer. He yearned to revisit his homeland but could never afford it.

Marilyn's mother, the former Thyra Linnet, was the daughter of Danish immigrants who lived in Tyler, Minnesota. She came to Pierre to work in a café. Short and plump, Thyra was conservative in her tastes and believed that nice women didn't wear lipstick.

Marilyn was the fourth of five children.

Though the family lived in town, they raised chickens and kept a cow or two for milk.

When Marilyn was nine years old, her mother died of breast cancer. From then on, she hated Mother's Day. If your mother was dead, you were expected to wear a white flower on that day. "I didn't like to call attention to it. It made me angry. I didn't want people to talk about it. Every place we'd go people would start talking about our mother. I didn't like them to keep singling us out as those poor Hansen kids."

There were few books in the house—only a Bible and a few Zane Grey westerns. But Mads Hansen made clear his admiration for educated people and told Marilyn that Bob Hipple, the editor of the Pierre *Capital Journal* newspaper, was the smartest man in town.

THERE WERE FEW firm rules in the Hansen home. Sunday school was mandatory. "Daddy would take us up to the little white Lutheran church in his black pickup truck and dump us off. He'd give us a nickel to put in the collection. He rarely went to church but insisted we did." He forbade his children to say "shut up" and gave them a nickel each time they went a week without uttering those words.

Marilyn was not athletic. Her legs were so long that some boys called her Spider. She played the piano ploddingly. She couldn't sing on key.

She wanted to excel at *something* and found that she could impress her teachers by reading more than the other children. She worked on her high school newspaper and was editor of the yearbook. "I was good at typing and although I was terribly shy I found I could step up and ask questions of people for the paper," she said later.

Her first job in journalism was as an assistant to the editor of an advertising sheet called the *Pierre Daily Reminder*. When there were blank spaces on the pages, Marilyn wrote short items to fill them and signed them as "Reminder Rat."

The editor of the *Capital Journal* gave her a summer job. Her duties included gathering snippets of local news. She proved resourceful in her reporting. One of her friends worked as a checkout girl at a grocery store. Marilyn persuaded her friend to quiz women who were buying larger-than-usual amounts of food. Were they expecting guests? That could be news for the *Capital Journal*.

When she was a sophomore in high school, in 1942, she found her father lying in his bed, dead from a heart attack at the age of 56. Her older brothers were serving in World War II, leaving the three Hansen sisters to fend for themselves. Marilyn worked as a dishwasher and later as a waitress at the St. Charles Hotel in Pierre.

THOUGH MONEY WAS tight, she enrolled at the University of South Dakota in Vermillion in 1944 and majored in journalism. Because most men were away during World War II, women had a rare chance to take leadership roles on campus. Marilyn became editor of the university's student newspaper, the *Volante*, in 1947. When Allen Neuharth returned from infantry service in the Army and enrolled at the university, she hired him as a sportswriter. He later became chief executive of Gannett Co. and founder of *USA Today*, but she would always remind him that he once worked for her.

When she had a summer job at the *Capital Journal* in Pierre in 1947, a friend mentioned Jack Hagerty, who worked for the United Press International news service. At five foot ten, Marilyn had trouble finding men of her stature. Her first question about Hagerty was how tall he was. Nearly six feet. Okay, she said, she would try dating him.

While working for the *American News* in Aberdeen in 1948, she had a job offer from a newspaper in Salt Lake City. It was far away and would have meant saying goodbye to Hagerty. Partly for those reasons, she turned it down. They married June 19, 1949, and had a honeymoon in Galveston, Texas. He was 30. She was 23.

The birth of her three children in the 1950s interrupted her career. Marilyn wrote stories occasionally on a freelance basis in her new hometown of Grand Forks, North Dakota.

Her professional life gradually revived as her children grew. She became the Dakota correspondent for the Fairchild trade papers and occasionally filled in for *Grand Forks Herald* staff members who were on vacation.

As a mom, she was unconventional. Driving her young children around town, she would always make the same remark upon seeing a pregnant woman crossing a street: "Look, lady, you could get knocked *down* too." Because we didn't know the meaning of the slang phrase "to get knocked up," we didn't understand what some people might consider an inappropriate remark. To discourage her children's habit of watching the "idiot box," she once announced that our TV set was broken. Only several days later did my sisters and I discover that it was merely unplugged.

In the mid-1960s, she began covering the Grand Forks school board for the *Herald*. She also began writing a column gathering together short items about people and events. "I never could think of a decent name for it so I just called it Behind the Scenes," she said.

Most of her columns were about other people, but a story she wrote about her own childhood memories was so popular that it was reprinted annually for decades:

## On Christmas Eve, I Must Go Home
### by Marilyn Hagerty

Excuse me, please. But it's Christmas Eve, and I must go home.

If only for five minutes and only in my thoughts, I have to go back on Christmas Eve. I haven't been there in person for many years. Still, I never have been away.

Every Christmas, there's a string of events that take me home. It starts when I hear children speaking pieces at church. Then it's the carols, the Christmas tree, the tinsel, the packages.

And in my mind, I snatch a few minutes to travel down Highway 14 in South Dakota once more. Around the curves and down that last big hill above the Missouri River.

I go in the back door.

I walk through the kitchen. The linoleum floor is cracked along the edges, but it is freshly scrubbed and waxed with Glo-coat for this night. As I put my things on the dining room table, I see the glow of lights from the tree in the front room.

I take my place there—close to the tree.

I see my brothers and sisters as children again. And in the big leather rocking chair, I see my dad. It's the moment I've been waiting for.

It always seemed on Christmas Eve everyone ate too slowly. It took too long to do the dishes. It was forever until they finished milking the cow and came back in the house. Then the boys always had to make one last quick shopping trip downtown to Vilas Drug.

Eventually, we open our presents. Daddy sits there holding some handkerchiefs and neckties in his big, rough hands. He has a shaving brush—made in Japan. With his Danish accent, he says, "We have too much. It is too much."

As I tear white tissue paper from a Shirley Temple doll and greedily scan the bottom of the tree for more presents, I think, "It is not too much for me."

Helen and Shirley fondle new sweaters and sniff their bubble bath. My brother Harley sits on the floor where the draft comes in under the front door. Walter sits beside him.

Most of the year, I consider Walter my personal enemy. I give him a pinch every time I have a chance. He slugs me back.

On Christmas Eve, with his hair combed and slicked down with oil, Walter looks almost like an angel. On Christmas Eve, nothing is too expensive for Walter's little sisters. He is generous with money he has earned delivering the *Capital Journal*.

We put on our coats and buckle up our overshoes before we start out for church. As we walk down the back road and up the hill this night seems different from all others.

Maybe it's because we girls get to go without long underwear on Christmas Eve. Maybe it's because we think we see the same star that guided the Wise Men.

It's cold and clear on Christmas Eve. Because we are early, we stand over the big heat register at the front of the church. Warm air blows up under our skirts. Later, some boys lucky to be chosen as shepherds have blankets draped around them. They get to come in the back door of the little Lutheran church and parade out the door beside the pulpit.

Five minutes is all I can take.

> It's time to come back to reality. This is the here and
> now. I have three children of my own. There's supper to
> fix before candlelight services at church.
> I wouldn't have it any other way.
> It's only a few minutes that I must tarry. I must go
> home each Christmas Eve.

ALONG WITH HER stories about local events and personalities, she wrote about restaurants. As she didn't consider herself an authority on cuisine, she refrained from criticizing the food. Instead, she wrote about the atmosphere and listed the most popular dishes along with their prices.

In early March 2012, when she was 85 years old and still working more or less full time, Marilyn turned in a routine story about a chain restaurant, the Olive Garden, which had recently opened in Grand Forks. That's when her life lurched into an entirely new dimension.

Internet wits stumbled upon the story and began mocking her for writing an earnest review of a chain restaurant that big city reviewers would acknowledge only with contempt, if at all. Within hours, newspaper reporters in Minneapolis and New York began calling Marilyn to ask what she made of all the snarky comments about her article.

She politely explained that she wasn't worried about it and didn't have time to scroll through "all this crap" on Twitter and Facebook.

This feisty response from a supposedly defenseless North Dakota grandmother endeared her to people around the world. Within days she was flying to New York to appear on national TV programs including *Today*, Anderson Cooper's talk show, and *Top Chef*, with Padma Lakshmi. Too busy with interview commitments in New York, she had to decline an invitation to appear on *The Tonight Show*.

Newspapers across the country wrote about her.

For the first few days of her celebrity, I waited for my editors at the *Wall Street Journal* to ask me to write about this phenomenon. After all, I knew more about it than any of the other reporters trying to explain my mother's sudden fame.

Finally, on a Saturday morning, I decided to write the story without being asked. I sat down at my laptop. Writing can be a slow and halting process, but this time the entire story came to me in a flash. I wrote as fast as my fingers could type.

It appeared on page one of the *Wall Street Journal* under the heading "When Mom Goes Viral":

> Some people pursue celebrity. Others stumble into it as they are rushing off to bridge club.
>
> My 85-year-old mom, Marilyn Hagerty, a newspaper columnist, is in the latter category. When she wrote a review of the new Olive Garden restaurant in Grand Forks, N.D., last week, she wasn't expecting anyone other than her thousands of loyal readers in North Dakota and northwestern Minnesota to take note. She didn't worry about how her story would play on Gawker, partly because she had never heard of Gawker.
>
> She's too busy to bother with blogs, Facebook or Twitter. She writes five articles a week for the *Grand Forks Herald.* Her specialties include local personalities, history and, yes, restaurants of high and low repute. Those whom she dubs in her column as "cheerful person of the week" consider it a high honor. She also cleans and maintains her house, cares for an unreliable dachshund, visits her eight grandchildren and volunteers at church.
>
> On Thursday, bloggers happened on her review of the Olive Garden, where she found the portions generous and the décor "impressive." Some wrote clever notes suggesting there might be some sort of irony in writing an unironic review about a chain restaurant like Olive Garden. Others, including media and news websites Gawker and Huffington Post, chimed in. Soon news hounds from Minneapolis, New York and even Fargo were calling Mom and demanding interviews. Basically,

they wanted to know whether she was for real and how she felt about being mocked all over the Internet.

She felt fine about it. But she didn't care to scroll through the thousands of Twitter and Facebook comments on her writing style. "I'm working on my Sunday column and I'm going to play bridge this afternoon," she explained, "so I don't have time to read all this crap." She didn't apologize for writing about a restaurant where many people like to eat. Her poise under fire endeared her to people who do read all that crap. Strangers started sending me emails about how much they loved my mom.

Her phone line was tied up, so I emailed her: "You've gone viral!"

She replied: "Could you tell me what viral means?"

Though she may not be hip to social media, Mom was always ready with the right quip. I remember a time when she and my father were posing for a portrait. The photographer asked Dad to raise his chin a bit. "Which one?" Mom deadpanned.

After 65 years of writing and editing for newspapers in both of the Dakotas, she didn't need to worry about leaving a mark on the world. She had already done that. More than a decade ago, she mused in one of her columns that it would be nice to have something named after her. It wouldn't have to be a grand building or a stadium, she wrote. A sewage-pumping station would do. The mayor of Grand Forks eventually complied. Visitors to the town will note the Marilyn Hagerty sewage facility, with a suitably engraved plaque in her honor, on Belmont Road.

Despite having secured her reputation for posterity, Mom retains her work ethic. When she takes a vacation, it is only after writing enough articles in advance to fill her daily space. She pays her own way at restaurants, rather than submitting expenses, so no one can say she

does reviews just to get free meals. When she was successfully treated for breast cancer two years ago, she used the
occasion to write a review of the hospital's food. It was
right up there with the cuisine at Olive Garden.

My mom has her own style of reviewing restaurants:
She doesn't like to say anything bad about the food. Her
regular readers read between the lines. If she writes
more about the décor than the food, you might want to
eat somewhere else.

Her Olive Garden review was actually mixed. She
said the "chicken Alfredo ($10.95) was warm and com-
forting on a cold day." She also noted that the restaurant
is "fashioned in Tuscan farmhouse style with a welcom-
ing entryway."

"As I ate," Mom wrote, "I noticed the vases and
planters with permanent flower displays on the ledges.
There are several dining areas with arched doorways.
And there is a fireplace that adds warmth to the décor."

Mom doesn't consider herself a food critic. She lives
in a college town with its share of local wiseguys. She
knows a thing or two about snide comments and con-
descension. As she told one interviewer, "I don't have
time to sit here and twit over whether some self-styled
food expert likes, or does not like, my column."

Her restaurant reviews, after all, are only a sideline.
She's more at home writing about people. One of her
best stories, in my view, was a 1974 profile of a bachelor
farmer, Magnus Skytland, who lived quite happily without electricity. He read by the light of a kerosene lamp
and sometimes serenaded himself on his violin. He
showed my mom his favorite horse, Sally, named after
a former girlfriend. "I've had three horses named Sally,"
he said.

The story about Sally is in a book of Mom's old columns, "Echoes," listed on Amazon as being worth $16

new or $15.50 used. Given the fleeting nature of Internet celebrity, this might be a good time to cash in. Still, I'm hanging on to my copy.

The only downside of the world's belated discovery of my mom is that she is too busy being interviewed on national television to play online Scrabble with me.

Mom, if you ever get time to read this, it's your move.

I NEVER EXPECTED to write a story about my mom for the front page of the *Wall Street Journal*. What really surprised me, though, was the reaction. I got email from readers all over the world, as far away as India. Everyone told me they loved my mother. Some wondered if she might adopt them.

> I never expected to write a story about my mom for the front page of the *Wall Street Journal*.

She was both amused and baffled by her unsought celebrity. "It's something that, if you tried to program it, you couldn't do it," she said.

To her surprise, her fame persisted as news organizations periodically called her up to comment on restaurants and related matters. Anthony Bourdain, the New York food writer and television personality, arranged to meet her. Bourdain was a complicated and sometimes tormented man who died by suicide some years later.

Something about my mom touched him. He persuaded Ecco/HarperCollins to publish a collection of her restaurant reviews, *Grand Forks: A History of American Dining in 128 Reviews*, released in 2013.

In his introduction to the book, Bourdain described her as "a good neighbor and good citizen first—and an entertainer second." He added: "She has a flinty, dry, very sharp sense of humor. She misses nothing. I would not want to play poker with her for money."

CHAPTER 21

# How Pros Cover
# Their Own Stories

THOUGH JOURNALISTS ARE NOT ALWAYS admired or loved, we do tend to learn the art of telling stories. This chapter presents a few examples of ways in which journalists have preserved their own life stories. I find them instructive.

MORT CRIM WAS a TV news anchorman in Philadelphia and Detroit. He looked and sounded so much like the stereotypical blow-dried blowhard TV anchorman that he became an inspiration for the *Anchorman* movies, featuring a pompously absurd character played by Will Ferrell and known as Ron Burgundy.

Crim thus might have gone down in history as little more than a joke. Instead, he took the narrative by the horns and, like his onetime mentor, Paul Harvey, told the rest of the story. It's an amazing and amusing tale. It is also a convoluted one. Crim keeps it coherent by concentrating on several themes: the evolution of his Christian faith, the unfolding of his career, and the true-to-life love story he lived with his wife.

In his 2021 book, *Anchored: A Journalist's Search for Truth*, Crim draws on humor, details, and anecdotes to evoke his boyhood in the small town of West Frankfort, Illinois, near the Kentucky and Missouri borders.

Black people weren't allowed in the town after dark. Crim was often left under the care of a grandmother, who didn't have time to keep a constant watch on him and occasionally leashed him to an elm tree with clothesline rope.

His father and one of his uncles were pastors in the Church of God denomination. "We had so many clergy in our family, we could have started our own denomination," Crim writes. But there were also former vaudeville entertainers in the family. Crim inherited a gift for sermonizing along with a knack for entertaining an audience. He was a holy ham.

As a teenager, he expected to follow his father into the ministry. Billed as the "Teenage Evangelist," he toured the Midwest with his Uncle Alvah Crim, dubbed "Brother Alvah." While Alvah strummed an electric guitar, young Mort squeezed gospel sounds out of his accordion.

At 16, he dropped out of high school for a spell to "hit the evangelistic trail as a solo act," as he put it. One motivation was that he was miserable at school, but Crim was able to justify the decision as a command from the Holy Spirit. "It's amazing how often God's call and divine direction seem to line up exactly with what we've already decided to do," he writes in his memoir.

Temptations loomed. At 17, he got a summer job at a country-music radio station in Blytheville, Arkansas, as a DJ earning 50 cents an hour. His radio name was Slim Crim.

Though he had begun to doubt his Christian faith, he enrolled in religious studies at Anderson University in Indiana. He dropped out of college to become a pastor at the Church of God in Portageville, Missouri. That gave him enough income to get married to his high school sweetheart, Nicki, when he was 19.

Six months later, he quit the church to create a Christian FM radio station, KRIM. To fill airtime, he played scratchy classical records borrowed from the local library and worn-out jukebox disks bought cheap. He didn't know he owed fees to royalty agencies for playing music. Between records, he and Nicki entertained listeners with stories they found in women's magazines and newspapers.

This enterprise collapsed within a few months. Crim doesn't make excuses: "I failed because I was cocky, arrogant, inexperienced, unfocused and grossly unprepared."

He found another preaching job but was increasingly troubled by his doubts over the literal truth of certain parts of the Bible. He couldn't bear the idea of mentioning those doubts to his devout parents. So he wrote to the radio announcer Paul Harvey for advice on whether to stay in the ministry or go into newscasting.

Harvey invited Crim to lunch in Chicago and said that he couldn't tell the young man which career to follow but that the broadcast news business needed people of integrity. That was enough for Crim, who resigned from the ministry and got a TV announcing job in Rockford, Illinois.

Faced with the draft, he enlisted in the Air Force in 1958. The Air Force helpfully assigned him to broadcasting work with the Armed Forces Radio Network. Matured by four years in the Air Force, he went to Northwestern University for a master's degree in journalism and found work at a New York radio station. ABC Radio Network later hired Crim and sent him to cover space launches, including the July 1969 moon landing. His career had taken a giant leap.

Eager to break into television, he sought advice from Walter Cronkite. (You may see a pattern here: Crim wasn't shy about seeking counsel from famous people.) Cronkite suggested leaving New York to work for a local station. That led to a TV anchorman job in Louisville, Kentucky. He was used to giving sermons. Talking to the camera came naturally. His face was on billboards. He befriended Harland Sanders, the founder of Kentucky Fried Chicken.

Crim discovered he didn't need a church or a pulpit to give sermons. Instead, in his spare time, he recorded 90-second inspirational programs syndicated to radio stations.

A bigger market beckoned: Philadelphia TV station KYW. Now he was a star in a larger town—and temporarily lost his moorings as the married father of two children. He let himself drift into an extramarital affair with a colleague and "unleashed a torrent of guilt and regret unlike anything I had ever felt." The affair "violated everything I believed about commitment and marriage," he writes.

He got counseling from a psychiatrist and was able to "confront the fact that I was broken, flawed, and capable of violating my own moral code." The counseling, he believes, saved his marriage and "quite possibly my life."

How much his wife knew is unclear. She didn't ask questions but "showed me in very personal terms what it means to love someone who doesn't deserve it."

The episode helped him distill what remained of his childhood faith: "Of all the beliefs I grew up with, one that remains true for me is this: God is love."

The second half of his TV career was at an NBC station in Detroit, where he helped turn around a floundering news operation and became a local star. The TV station paid for a hairstylist and a clothing consultant. Two local radio DJs recorded a song called "Mort Crim's Hairspray."

Detroit's diversity of religion and culture inspired him: "I saw in this kaleidoscope of beliefs a profound truth: loving God and loving each other are two aspects of the same experience."

In his middle age, he writes, "I was beginning to understand God not as a riddle to be solved or a question to be answered, but as a presence to be accepted."

For several years in the early 1980s, he filled in for Paul Harvey on his radio show when Harvey was traveling.

In 1989, his wife, Nicki, died of cancer. Crim was 54. He admits to drinking too much in the early months of his grief. Partly for his children's sake, he pulled himself together. Two years after Nicki's death, he married Irene Bowman Miller. He retired from full-time journalism at 65 but still recorded syndicated radio programs.

Jack White, a Detroit-raised rock musician, used one of Crim's sonorous radio sermonettes as an intro for his song "Little Acorns," recorded by the White Stripes.

Crim's memoir circles back repeatedly to the evolution of his Christian faith from a literal reading of the Bible to something more universal and accepting of ambiguity: "As for life after death," he writes, "my faith gives me a calm assurance that whatever comes next will be okay, and any thought I might give to the hereafter would be mere speculation."

After reading his book, I called Crim in April 2021 to learn how he managed to tell his own tale. I learned that even for a professional writer like Crim, it was a challenge. He worked on the project off and on for five years. At first, the book was little more than a string of anecdotes. Friends advised him to tie the story together with the theme of his search to reconcile the fundamentalist religious faith of his childhood with his discovery of a more complicated world of adulthood.

Then it was a matter of deciding what to include. The toughest question he faced was whether he should write about the brief extramarital affair. Though the colleague and his first wife were both dead, he still needed to think about how his children would react to his making such a confession publicly. He talked it over with both of them. Both urged him to include this painful episode. "They didn't see how I could write honestly without including it," Crim said. They also didn't want him to depict himself as a saint.

"Every single human being alive has a story that's worth telling," Crim said. "Not everybody has the desire to tell it." For those who do, Crim provides a model of vivid writing and frank descriptions of his ups and downs.

So does Peter R. Kann.

Kann won a Pulitzer Prize for reporting and served as chief executive of Dow Jones & Co., the publisher of the *Wall Street Journal* and other newspapers, from 1991 to 2006. Even so, he could walk down almost any street in America with no risk of being recognized. Outside the world of newspapers, his name would rarely ring even the faintest bell.

So who wanted his memories? His children did. They prodded him to write his life story and so, one day in retirement, he sat on a beach in Malibu and started putting his memories down on paper. He ended up producing a slender volume for, as he put it, "my children, my grandchildren and possibly some generations yet to come."

The book is not available for sale, but I was lucky enough to receive a copy and found it an excellent model. It contains the basic information needed for any obituary his family may one day wish to publish, along with the larger story of why and how he became a journalist, and the surprising things that happened along the way.

Peter Robert Kann was born in 1942 and grew up in Princeton, New Jersey. His parents, both born in Vienna, were refugees from Nazi-controlled Austria. His father was a professor of history at Rutgers University. His mother was an office manager.

Perhaps influenced by his father, who wrote books about Austrian history, Kann took an early interest in finding out what was happening in the world and explaining it to others. At first, the world he covered was very small. At age 10, he began publishing his own newspaper, the *Jefferson Road Snooper*, covering news and gossip in his suburban neighborhood. His mother did the typing. A few dozen neighbors paid five cents an issue. One neighbor, Kann recalled, "shooed me off his porch by saying, 'I don't need no snoopers.' That too was reported in the next issue."

He was editor of his junior high and high school papers and had summer jobs at the *Princeton Packet* newspaper. One of his early idols was George Orwell, "who notably never used a big or obscure word when a short and common one would do."

At age 16, he wrote a story for the *Packet* exposing the squalid living conditions of Mexican migrant farmhands working in the fields near Princeton. The *Packet* was owned by Barney Kilgore, publisher of the *Wall Street Journal*. Kilgore liked Kann's work and suggested he apply for a job at the *Journal* after college.

In 1960, he enrolled in Harvard. "I was not a serious student," he confesses. He was more interested in working for the *Harvard Crimson* newspaper, where his colleagues included Michael Crichton and

Donald Graham, future publisher of the *Washington Post*. One summer he worked as an intern at the *Wall Street Journal*.

After graduating from Harvard, in 1964, he wanted to be a reporter in Asia, a place that struck him as remote, exotic, and abounding in beautiful women. He sent letters of application to English-language newspapers in Hong Kong. They didn't bother to reply.

So Kann accepted a job at the Pittsburgh bureau of the *Wall Street Journal*. "My job was unexciting, at least for someone who lacked passion for heavy metals," he wrote. He must have done something right, however, because after nine months the paper promoted him to its Los Angeles bureau. There he covered the movie industry, had a blind date with Marlo Thomas, and wrote a story about a woman who had seen *The Sound of Music* 600 times.

He kept asking for a transfer to Asia and was so set on that goal that he turned down a chance to join the London bureau. In the fall of 1967, at age 24, he became the *Journal*'s first resident reporter in Vietnam, covering the war.

To differentiate his work, he sought to write about how the war affected the Vietnamese people rather than focusing mainly on American soldiers in combat. He was the only reporter to infiltrate and report on a secret CIA program using Cambodian mercenaries to make raids on the Vietcong. He had an eye for details: In a pile of helmets and personal effects of recently killed American soldiers, he spotted a tattered book, *Applying to College and Getting In*. The book's owner, he wrote, "would never be getting there."

Later he became a roving Asian correspondent, based in Hong Kong. An early marriage there didn't work out. In Balochistan, he witnessed camel races and a striptease in which the climax was the flash of an ankle. He won a Pulitzer Prize for his coverage of the Bangladesh war in 1971.

The greatest joy of his career was wandering in places overlooked by other journalists and writing his own quirky style of story. That chapter of his life ended as a result of a suggestion he made to his bosses in New York. Though he wasn't particularly interested in business, he saw that Asia would become a much more important part of the global economy and urged Dow Jones to invest there. In the 1970s, he proposed an Asian edition of the *Journal*. To his surprise, the bosses agreed to try out his idea and named him editor and publisher of the new edition at the age of 33.

He became what he never aspired to be: a business executive. "It was not nearly as much fun as roaming Waziristan or the Hindu Kush, but there was some appeal to it," he wrote. There was no easy escape from the promotions that followed, taking him to New York and up through the ranks to the top of the company.

In some ways, his timing was fortunate. The period from about 1980 until 2000 was a golden age for newspapers, and especially the *Journal*. As advertising and circulation grew, the *Journal* expanded from one section to three and sometimes four. It was admired and won Pulitzer Prizes.

"I sometimes wondered then, and have wondered since, how much credit I actually deserved for any of this success," he wrote in his memoir. "Most decisions I made required ordinary common sense more than extraordinary brilliance or creativity." (Contrast this refreshing and unfeigned modesty with the exaggerated praise found in too many obituaries written by family members.)

At one company meeting at a resort, Kann organized a late-night golf cart race and drove his cart into a pond. It sank and had to be removed the next day with a crane.

His job became much less fun when the company's financial-data arm, Telerate, fell behind its rivals and dragged down overall corporate performance. "Each so-called progression in my career had taken me further and further from what I most loved—journalism," he wrote. Meetings bored him; he hated being locked into the corporate schedule, unable to roam at will.

He made some good calls. When the online version of the *Journal* was launched in 1996, he insisted on charging for access. Some colleagues said, "Peter, don't you know the internet is free?" He thought a free online version would undercut the print edition and create too much reliance on uncertain ad revenue. Many other newspapers gave away their stories online for years before adopting the same sort of paywall put up by the *Journal* from the start.

Kann's story shows how career plans adopted in youth rarely work out as forecast. "I always knew I wanted to be a journalist, and I also wanted to live in Asia. But I never had a plan beyond that—no grand strategy for my future," he wrote.

It turned out he didn't need one. When it was time to tell his life story, he had plenty of good material—and the self-confidence required to admit a few mistakes.

LIFE STORIES CAN be very short. Nora Ephron (1941–2012), a former journalist now better known as the author of the novel *Heartburn* and the screenplay for *When Harry Met Sally*, summed up her life in a comic essay, "The story of my life in 3,500 words or less." It's included in her 2006 book, *I Feel Bad About My Neck*. Rather than methodically recording her whole life story, she selects moments or incidents that sparked insights. Sample chapter title: "My Life Changes". That chapter in full: *I write a magazine article about having small breasts. I am now a writer.*

> Life stories can be very short.

Few could write so succinctly, but Ephron showed how much can sometimes be packed into a few words. Read your draft carefully and delete any words that are merely taking up space.

# CHAPTER 22

# Tom Vartabedian, Obituary Hero

Dᴜʀɪɴɢ Toᴍ Vᴀʀᴛᴀʙᴇᴅɪᴀɴ's 50-ʏᴇᴀʀ newspaper career at the *Gazette* in Haverhill, Massachusetts, he wrote stories about city hall, sports, and personalities, including a profile of a woman who collected pencils. The stories he found most meaningful, Tom told me, were the obituaries.

He wrote thousands of them. In each one, he tried to reveal character, not just dates and titles and honors. "If somebody was kind to animals and rescued stray cats from the Merrimack River, I would use that as the lead for that person's obit. You have to grab readers right off the bat," Tom told me. He snapped his fingers. "You can't be trite about it."

What about people who avoided the spotlight and never made even the local news? "Sometimes those make the best obituaries, like the guy who coached little league baseball for 25 years," Tom said. He recalled a friend who served as a church deacon for 61 years. "Would I write about that? You bet I would."

I met Tom in the spring of 2016, when I was new to the obituary beat. He was 75 at the time, a roundish man with a moustache, a fringe of close-cropped gray hair, and a constellation of age spots on his forehead. He had recently been diagnosed with stage four gastrointestinal cancer.

Around the time he received that diagnosis, he also received an invitation. Haverhill's Council on Aging asked him to teach a short course on how to write your own obituary. He loved the idea. "Wouldn't it be wonderful if we wrote these stories when people were alive, to enjoy them?" he said. "I often think about that."

Around 30 people registered for 10 hours of instruction from Tom over several weeks. I attended one of the meetings.

Tom's message would become my mantra: "Don't leave anything to chance—the chance that somebody else makes a debacle of it." Friends and family mean well, but they may skip a cherished memory or accomplishment.

You need to leave a script.

Tom started by giving general encouragement and persuading his students—mostly aged 60 and older—that writing their stories was not a trivial or vain exercise. "It's deeds, not tombstones, that are the true monuments of us as people," he said.

Then he encouraged his students to read excerpts from drafts of their own life stories.

One of his students, a retired court clerk, had a question. "I don't want to sound like I'm bragging," she told Tom, but she wondered: Would it be okay to mention her two bowling trophies?

"That would be perfectly appropriate," Tom said. "Don't think that your life is any more insignificant than anyone else's."

A former school caretaker named Bill had typed his first draft on a single sheet of yellow legal paper. He didn't own a computer, so he used a typewriter.

Bill wanted his obituary to note that the school where he was caretaker once honored him with a "Mr. Bill Day." But he couldn't remember what year that was.

Don't worry about the exact date, Tom advised. "Nobody is going to call you on the carpet. You can get away with a lot of things in an obituary."

Bill also was including a few words about how he helped out at a thrift shop and served on a committee that oversaw hiking trails. To convey his love of animals, he wrote, "His soul will stop at Pet Heaven, before going to Heaven."

Bill realized that his death was unlikely to be page-one news. Still, he hoped his obituary would be read by at least one person—his estranged sister. "My sister doesn't know me," he told the class. "I'm writing this so she will know me."

One of the other students wrote about her pet quail and a trip to Lourdes. Another mentioned her service as a voting clerk and membership in a polka club. A third listed missionary trips to Mexico and Uganda.

Another student, who was 82, said she was skeptical at first about the idea of writing her own story. "I said, 'Who cares? I'm dead. It doesn't make any difference.'" Then she started writing, partly for the sake of her eight children.

"I said to my children, 'You really don't know me as a person, my core values. You know me as mama, nana, whatever, but I was an individual; I was a person, before I became a mother.'"

As a teenage mother in Alabama, she cleaned houses during the day and finished high school with evening courses before becoming the first person in her family to finish college—and then earning two master's degrees.

She included this message: "If you wish to remember me, do a kind deed, show love, give a smile or words of encouragement to someone who needs it."

A student named Julie wrote that she had taught Sunday school and sung in several choirs. Her draft obituary noted: "She did not sing great. However, it was her greatest joy."

Even as he taught others to write their obituaries, Tom Vartabedian was writing his own on a computer in a home office whose walls were decorated with awards and medals from athletic events of the distant past.

Tom had plenty of material for his story. He was the son of Armenian immigrants who ran a coffee shop. He majored in journalism at

Boston University, studied abroad for a year at a monastery in Vienna, won newspaper-writing awards and racquetball prizes, led Armenian community programs, brought up three children, and climbed "each of the tallest peaks in New England, including Mount Washington six times."

The first sentence of his draft obituary described him as "an award-winning *Haverhill Gazette* writer-photographer for 50 years and Armenian community activist." It said he died "following a courageous battle with cancer."

That wording should be justified, Tom told me, "because I would say my battle was a courageous battle, at least I want to think it is. If I'm using a superlative that might be out of place, I don't really think it is."

There were other things he wanted his family and friends to know or remember. Since 1970, he had written a newspaper column called Poor Tom's Almanac. He won the American Cancer Society's Sword of Hope Award for writing about the disease. As a member of the Armenian Genocide Education Committee of Merrimack Valley, he visited high schools to talk about genocide and human rights.

He was a leader in the Kenoza Camera Club and donated his camera collection to the photography department at Haverhill High School.

He hadn't shown the draft to his wife of 51 years, Nancy, a retired schoolteacher. She might nitpick, or even delete parts of his story, he said.

Nancy had her own view on obituaries. She told me her children would be perfectly capable of writing hers. In any case, she said, "after I'm gone, it doesn't matter. They can write whatever they want."

I liked Nancy. I could tell she kept Tom grounded. But I thought Tom was right in this case.

After he finished writing his story, Tom felt relieved. "I took care of business," he said. "I took care of business that had to be resolved. After it was done, it was like an albatross was off my back. I had written probably the most important story of my life. It was my story."

I lingered with him outside his house before getting back into my rented car and heading for the airport. "I don't fear death. I don't welcome death, but I don't fear death," Tom said. "I'm hoping I'll go another three or four years."

As a reporter, he was still interested in learning. "I'm really curious as to what's on the other side. What's heaven like?" he said. "Hopefully, I'll end up there."

Tom died on November 12, 2016, six months after I met him. The *New York Times* didn't note his passing. But a local newspaper published the obituary Tom wrote for himself, in full—just as he wanted it.

CHAPTER 23

# *Fishers of Men*

$R$ON AND AL LINDNER WERE not trained to write. They were fishermen.

And yet they set down their life stories indelibly in a 2015 book, *Reflections at First Light*, that doubles as a memoir and devotional.

Fans of TV fishing shows knew about the Lindners long ago. The brothers liked to say they taught the "algebra of angling": fish + location + presentation = success.

I learned about them only in late 2020, when Ron died at the age of 86. Here is a short version of their tale:

In the mid-1960s, Ron and his younger brother, Al, moved from their native Chicago to Minnesota. Their ambition was to make a living out of their obsession: fishing.

The Lindners found work as fishing guides on a cluster of lakes near Brainerd in central Minnesota. Eventually, they also sold the Lindy Rig, a fishing lure Ron Lindner devised to catch walleye and other fish.

After selling their Lindy Rig business in 1974, they launched *In-Fisherman* magazine and branched into books, television, and radio shows.

Though Ron Lindner's dream of living off his hobby came true, alcoholism nearly destroyed him. He credited his recovery to Alcoholics Anonymous and an evangelist who redirected him into a life focused on his Christian faith.

And so the Lindner brothers became fishers of men, as described in the Gospels, and spent much of their time sharing their faith.

In their book, the brothers recalled childhood summers at a lake cabin owned by their paternal grandparents near Hayward, Wisconsin. Ron, a decade older than Al, persuaded his little brother to dig up the worms, repair the tackle, and load the boat. "He told me everyone starts out as a 'worm boy' apprentice, and for years I believed him," Al Lindner wrote.

Ron served in the Army and spent a dozen years working on road-construction crews, leaving time for fishing only on weekends. When Al returned in 1966 from Army service in Vietnam, the brothers began their work as fishing guides.

Ron Lindner's Lindy Rig became a hit in the late 1960s, and the brothers set up Lindy Tackle Co. to make it. The rig features a sinker shaped like a shoehorn and is designed to slide through and over rocks without getting snagged.

After selling the Lindy Tackle business, the brothers wanted to produce their own TV series. They pitched the idea to Ted Turner's WTBS broadcasting outlet. WTBS showed interest but finally didn't take the bait. Ron Lindner, who was supporting seven children, had already spent much of the money he got from the sale of the tackle company. He worried about going broke.

"I was in a manic state and started drinking heavily," he wrote. The breaking point came on a spring weekend in Minneapolis, where he was attending a trade show. Ron went on a bender, forgot where he had parked his car, and woke up in a hotel room. He didn't know what day it was.

A few days later, at the suggestion of his wife, Dolores, he attended a revival meeting led by Lowell Lundstrom in Crosby, Minnesota. The evangelist summoned those who wished to accept Jesus as their savior. "I jumped out of my seat and almost ran to the stage," Ron wrote.

With their TV plans on hold, the brothers decided to try selling a series of fishing study guides. Helped by their wives, they prepared a brochure and began mailing it out. The goal was to find 1,000 sub-scribers to pay for the guides in advance. Within a few months, they had sold 17,000 subscriptions.

In 2020, Ron's health was failing fast. In the fall, Al took his big brother fishing at a secret spot near Brainerd. "We caught a whole bunch of smallmouth bass," Al told me later. He recalled Ron saying that it might be his last fishing trip. It was.

A few weeks later, after enduring cancer treatments and catching pneumonia and then COVID-19, Ron told his brother, "Al, no more hospitals, man." Ron wanted to die at home. He did.

The Lindner brothers, fishing guides turned spiritual guides, told their story as a parable and expres-sion of their faith. A life story does

**A life story does not require a broader theme.**

not require a broader theme, but the Lindners found one way to offer a more universal message.

# CHAPTER 24

# How I'm Writing My Own Story (and Some of the Dumb Stuff I Did)

IF I DIE TOMORROW MY family has permission to publish the following notice in a local newspaper:

> James Robert "Bob" Hagerty, a newspaper reporter and editor on three continents for more than 40 years, died (note to family: please supply date and circumstances, omitting any gruesome details) at the age of ??.
>
> His wife, Lorraine, and two children allowed him to indulge weaknesses for softball, pickleball, books, beer, music, and dachshunds.
>
> Bob spent too much of his time on such trifles as earning a living and ensuring his own comforts. On the plus side, he tried to be friendly and helpful, tutored immigrants seeking to improve their English, volunteered in elder-care programs, raised money for a public library by organizing beer-tasting events, founded a Scrabble club, and managed senior softball teams.
>
> He showed an obsessive streak by keeping 5,000 baseball cards collected in his youth, and later adding

thousands of records and compact discs, along with innumerable books wedged into every spare nook of his house. Some of those books crossed oceans six times during his relocations.

He once hitchhiked 450 miles overnight from Duluth to Bismarck. He rode trains from Bangkok to Singapore and from Abidjan to Ouagadougou.

The third of three children, he was born in Minneapolis. His mother, Marilyn Hansen Hagerty, was a newspaper reporter who unintentionally attracted national renown when her review of an Olive Garden restaurant went viral on the internet in 2012. His father, Jack Hagerty, wrote for the United Press International news wire and later was editor of the North Dakota *Grand Forks Herald*.

The family moved to Grand Forks when Bob was about a year old.

Around age five, Bob made his debut in journalism by creating a very short-lived neighborhood newspaper called *Worm Killers*. With his sister Carol, he later produced the weekly *Neighborhood Star*, for which 15 or 20 subscribers paid five cents every other week, which worked out to two and a half cents per copy.

His early career goals included cowboy, major league baseball player, architect, or president of a small tropical island. All of those visions faded when he was about 15 and saw the high school newspaper produced by a team led by his other sister, Gail. Deeply impressed that teenagers could create such a professional-looking publication, he was determined to do the same. He served for two years as editor of his high school paper, the *Riders Digest*, and decided to make a career in journalism.

His other work experiences, including french fry duty at McDonald's, confirmed his preference for reporting, photography, and editing. As a teenager, he worked briefly at Kmart, where he was assigned to assemble bicycles. He wishes to apologize belatedly to anyone who bought a bicycle he assembled; he trusts that the statute of limitations applies.

Bob attended the University of North Dakota, where he was editor of the student newspaper and majored in economics and foosball. His father alerted him to an internship program sponsored by the Newspaper Fund, backed by Dow Jones & Co., publisher of the *Wall Street Journal*. Bob obtained an internship and spent the summer of 1976 in New York as a very junior copydesk hand, editing and writing headlines for stories that typically were one or two inches long. He also had summer internships at newspapers in Bismarck, North Dakota, and Duluth, Minnesota.

During his final year at the University of North Dakota, he applied for jobs at more than 40 newspapers in the Midwest and Rocky Mountain states. One of those newspapers, in Moscow, Idaho, asked him to obtain a recommendation from the *Wall Street Journal*. When Bob called his former supervisor at the *Journal*, John Kelleher, to request a letter of recommendation, Kelleher instead offered him a job in New York.

Though he wanted to be a reporter, Bob joined the *Wall Street Journal* as a copy editor in April 1978. Fifteen months later he volunteered for a transfer to the new Asian edition of the *Wall Street Journal* in Hong Kong, even though he had only a vague idea of where Hong Kong was.

He expected to work abroad for two or three years and ended up spending more than two decades in Asia and Europe, working for the *Wall Street Journal* and the *International Herald Tribune*. At various points in his career, he was based in New York, Hong Kong, Paris, London, Brussels, Atlanta, and Pittsburgh. He liked Brussels best.

He served diligently, with mixed results, as managing editor of the *Asian Wall Street Journal* and as London bureau chief of the *Wall Street Journal*. He much preferred his long periods as a reporter.

He wrote about topics including the oil industry, currency and bond markets, residential real estate, and manufacturing. In his spare time, he also wrote *The Fateful History of Fannie Mae*, a book explaining the origins of U.S. government subsidies of home mortgages. During his later years at the *Wall Street Journal*, he found his true calling: writing obituaries, or "life stories" as he preferred to call them. That led him to write another book, *Yours Truly*.

"I write obituaries," he often said. "If you get a phone call from me, it probably isn't a good sign."

Bob regretted getting married too young, at age 21, and the length of time it took him to end the marriage after he stopped wanting it to continue—a delay that mainly reflected his genuine and pathetic inability to make a decision, but was unfair to his first wife. While living in Hong Kong for a second time, in the 1990s, he met Lorraine Li, office manager of the *Asian Wall Street Journal*. They married in 1996 and had two children, James Lee and Carmen Lee.

Bob's advice included: Don't hold grudges, don't believe everything you think, and don't forget to write your own story.

THAT'S THE SHORT form of my life story. As for the longer version—written for my own amusement and the possible interest of a few other people—I haven't finished it. I'm still working in spare moments on what has turned into a long-term project, frequently interrupted by other projects, including the present task of writing about writing my own life story.

Yet I vow to finish the job.

What to include? I can't write down everything I remember. That would be tedious, for me and my readers. So I try to choose what I find amusing, instructive, or helpful in explaining why my life turned out as it did.

One thing I'm likely to keep is a passage on my earliest memories:

> My first memory is of nailing soda-bottle caps into the interior walls of our garage and pretending they were radio knobs. I had a companion across the street, Mark Gottschalk. We had picnic lunches in a small clump of trees at the back of his lawn, alongside an alley, a place we called the Old Fort. We pretended to be World War II soldiers. It was the early 1960s, and war movies were popular. We had plastic war toys, including guns and even Nazi helmets. In retrospect, it seems odd that, just 15 years after the Holocaust, some American parents were comfortable seeing their children dress up as Nazi soldiers. Of course, they also gave us candy cigarettes and let us play with firecrackers, including some powerful enough to blow off a finger. In those days, most parents did not agonize over how their actions or omissions might scar children for life. For the most part, I benefited from their loose supervision.

Those memories evoke elements of early-1960s life that may surprise my children. I also hope to convey to them that my early days in school were not promising:

> For my first few years of grade school, I was a poor to middling student. On a report card, my kindergarten teacher, Barbara Spicer, wrote in her lovely cursive script that I was "reluctant to volunteer information during

discussion periods." She did not specify what sort of information I was expected to "volunteer." Having seen war movies, I perhaps knew that, if captured, I should provide only name, rank, and serial number.

On that same report card, under the heading "Conforms to reasonable standards of cleanliness and health habits," I improved from "average development" in the third period to "commendable development" in the fourth.

For a time, I believed that if I could not be one of the best students, being one of the worst was an equally desirable distinction. My highest aspiration was to be one of the class clowns. Gradually I learned to pay attention, part of the time, and deliver what the teachers demanded. To my surprise, it wasn't very hard. I silently thrilled to the praise of teachers and craved more. From the fifth grade on, I was an excellent student. One thing I discovered was that teachers tended to be more animated and enthusiastic when presenting the parts of the lesson they considered most important. Those were the ones I copied into my notes and studied. Writing down everything the teacher said would only clutter my mind and make it harder to remember what mattered on the test.

MY LOVE OF nature did not come from my parents, who disliked exposing themselves to insects, snakes, or any greenery wilder than a golf fairway. We lived in a town surrounded by wheat, potato, and sugar beet fields. No raw nature intruded on our daily lives. The YMCA came to my rescue:

> In the summer, we joined YMCA camping trips at nearby lakes and state parks. While the Boy Scouts marched along nature trails and learned to light a fire by rubbing two stones together, we lolled around at the campsite and started our fires by throwing a highway

flare or a cup of motor oil into a stack of soggy wood. It was Woodstock—without the topless girls or music—for 12-year-old boys. One of our favorite activities was catching frogs. Once we camped alongside Boy Scouts and observed an uneasy truce with them until they set off on an early morning march. We then stole their flag, tossed dozens of live frogs into their tents, zipped the tents back up tightly, and boarded our bus to return home to badly-needed baths.

AT SOME POINT every child learns that some, if not all, adults are insane and perhaps dangerous. My moment of awakening seems worth recording:

Our junior high school gym teacher was nicknamed "Moose." For gym class, boys were segregated from girls. The boys were required to wear a uniform of white T-shirt, gym shorts, white socks, and an athletic supporter, or "jockstrap," rather than underpants. Teenage boys, of course, are often forgetful and might neglect to bring their freshly laundered gym clothing to school. Moose would not tolerate these lapses.

We frequently began our gym class with a "jockstrap inspection." All of us lined up like soldiers on a parade ground. Gen. Moose strutted down the line and required each of us in turn to lower our shorts enough so that he could see whether we were wearing our jockstraps, and not trying to get by with normal underwear. Those who forgot their jockstraps were required by Moose to bend over so he could smack them on the bottom with a wooden paddle. Afterwards in the shower room, we would see the resulting bright-red welts. I never forgot my jockstrap.

ANOTHER RITE OF passage is learning whether, and if so how, to drink alcohol. Many people go through this stage in high school. I waited for college and then had an accelerated course:

> On one of my first evenings as a college student, I followed others to a fraternity, where kegs of beer were set out on the front lawn with no attempt at concealment. I had a few glasses of beer and felt for the first time the euphoria of mild inebriation. Of course, I tumbled straight into the delusion of thinking that if a little was great, a lot would be even better.
>
> On one occasion, after drinking beer chased with shots of tequila in a dormitory room, I walked out to the lounge with friends. Instead of walking around the sofa as usual, I decided to leap over it. At the apex of my leap, my head smashed into a heating duct. After crash-landing on the tile floor, I felt no pain but noticed blood was gushing from my head. My roommate drove me to an emergency room, where seven stitches closed the wound. The next day I had to explain to my mother why I had been to the hospital.
>
> "You weren't drinking, were you?"
>
> "Oh, no!"
>
> Surely she did not believe me. Wisely she did not press the matter. The lesson had been learned.
>
> I never again drank tequila. And soon I learned to stop drinking as soon as I felt a certain fuzziness in my head that signaled an impending loss of self-control. My fear of hangovers exceeded my desire for any euphoria or oblivion that alcohol might bring.

I WILL INCLUDE a note about hitchhiking, something that was normal when I was a young man but now would be considered bizarre:

On a Friday evening in the summer of 1975, while I was working as an intern for a newspaper in Duluth, I suddenly decided to visit a girlfriend in Bismarck, 450 miles to the southwest. Neither of us had a telephone, so I could not announce my impending visit. I walked to a gas station, and almost immediately a truck driver named Merlin Hintz let me climb into his cab. He had 25 tons of cement in the back and a pack of cigarettes up front. Merlin and I chatted half the night as we rode through the pine forests of northern Minnesota and into the plains of eastern North Dakota. Around 3 a.m., Merlin dropped me off at a truck stop in Valley City, North Dakota, as far as he could take me, still 135 miles short of my destination. It seemed like a bad idea to hitchhike in the dark, so I sat in the truck stop café until dawn before returning to the roadside. A man hauling bread drove me the rest of the way to Bismarck.

The girlfriend was surprised to see me but seemed pleased. If she had taken up with someone else, it would have been a long trip back to Duluth.

People were far less wary of strangers in those days. During another long-distance hitchhiking trip, a car driven by a young man, accompanied by his girlfriend, stopped to pick me up. The young couple told me they were tired and asked me to drive their car while they napped in the back seat. So I did.

I MISS THAT youthful spontaneity, that willingness and ability to drop everything at the first sign of a potential adventure.

In the mid-1970s, I worked as an assistant to the University of North Dakota's photographer. My job was to mix chemicals, develop film, and make prints. While I was working in the darkroom one afternoon, the chief photographer, Jerry, got a phone call from a woman who said she needed publicity pictures. Jerry wasn't interested and so handed the phone to me. I agreed to meet her at the cheap motel where she was staying.

When I arrived at the motel, I met Diana Love (not her real name, I suspect), who was doing a striptease act at a local bar that week. Diana asked whether I had ever taken nude pictures. "Well, not exactly," I stammered, "but…" Willing myself to remain calm, I drove her out to the university photo studio. Diana had a trunk full of props, including a feather boa. She casually disrobed as I fumbled with the camera, tripod, and lights.

In the middle of our shooting session, the head of the university's audiovisual department happened to open the studio door. He closed it very quickly, without a word, and never asked me for an explanation.

Diana paid me $20 for the pictures. She asked for the negatives as well. I gave her an envelope full of negatives from a recent picnic and kept the ones featuring her. (Diana, if by chance you are reading this, I owe you an apology and am happy to forward the negatives to you, if I can find them in my attic.)

I mounted a profile shot of the busty Ms. Love on black cardboard and took it to the next meeting of the Grand Forks Camera Club as my entry in the monthly photo contest. The other members, mostly middle-aged men, entered pictures of old cars, sagging barns, or rusting farm equipment. My picture won the first-prize ribbon.

> A father's life story, recorded for his children, should include lessons he learned from his mistakes.

A FATHER'S LIFE story, recorded for his children, should include lessons he learned from his mistakes. I've been blessed with an abundance of those. I include the following

story because it shows I was willing to go to great lengths on a whim
for a bit of adventure, but was also liable to squander an opportunity
through my impetuous decisions:

> The *International Herald Tribune* sent me to Nigeria for
> a week in 1985 to report on the country's oil-based econ-
> omy. As part of my preparation, I read Chinua Achebe's
> novel *Things Fall Apart* and his political lament *The
> Trouble With Nigeria*. His blunt, concise style of writing
> appealed to me.
>
> I found the capital city of Lagos a sweltering chaos.
> In roads choked with slow-moving traffic, vendors
> walked between the cars and waved merchandise for
> sale—food, telephones, toilet paper, whatever you
> might need. Long before the invention of the smart-
> phone, you could accomplish your weekly shopping
> while stuck in traffic.
>
> At loose ends over the weekend, I decided to seek
> out Achebe and solicit his latest insights on Nigeria's
> troubles. I knew he worked several hundred miles away
> at a university in Nsukka, a town in Biafra, a Nigerian
> region devastated by famine and civil war in the late
> 1960s. In those pre-email days, phone service was unre-
> liable. It proved impossible to give the author any
> warning of my intended visit.
>
> I bought a domestic airline ticket from Lagos to
> Enugu. At the Lagos airport, I learned that there were no
> boarding gates. Instead, you walked out onto the tarmac
> and wandered among the airplanes until you found the
> one going to your destination. I got the last seat.
>
> From Enugu, I took a taxi some 40 miles to Nsukka,
> passing scores of rusted cars abandoned by the road.
> When we reached Nsukka, the driver and I began asking
> people we encountered in the dusty streets how to find
> Achebe's home. Each person we met strove, with words

and gestures, to explain the unexplainable, then finally got into the taxi to direct us from a position of greater comfort. Before long, several guides were squeezed into the taxi with me. Eventually, we found the right house, surrounded by flower beds.

I rapped at the door. Achebe appeared. "I have found you!" I gushed.

Achebe did not share my enthusiasm. He informed me that he was too busy to grant me more than five minutes of his time. Stunned, I declined his offer.

I slunk back to the taxi. Did Achebe not realize the trouble and expense I had taken to reach his home? Was it not his vocation to explain his homeland to the rest of the world?

Later I realized that, from Achebe's perspective, I was an uninvited pest, liable to ask him naïve questions and quote him out of context. Perhaps he also felt, rightly, that his books spoke for themselves. If I had been wiser, I would have accepted his offer of a few minutes. Who knows, it might have stretched to hours. Surely I would have learned something.

EVENTUALLY, I BECAME a manager of reporters and copy editors. For the most part, I didn't love being a manager. I yearned to get back to reporting and writing my own stories. Yet my brief career as a manager did give me insights into human nature:

> When I was managing editor of the *Asian Wall Street Journal* in the mid-1990s, I received job application letters almost daily. Recently, in our attic, I found a file containing my favorites.
>
> A woman in Vermont opened her application letter with refreshing frankness: "I have left my husband and want to relocate immediately to the other side of the world."

Winnie of Hong Kong believed a job as a news assistant would "enable me to perceive variety of experience whereby in defense from any subsequent change in phenomenal paradigms and the like."

Sam of London informed us that he had "canoeing skills."

Seeking an editing job, Chris explained his writing technique: "I strive to locate the whole within the fragment and the fragment in the whole, to establish an organizational structure ... and to guide the reader over interstitial paths with distinct points of departure and arrival."

Delwar of Dhaka wrote: "I pray and hope that your gracious honor would be kind enough to appoint me as your correspondent for Bangladesh."

From a 29-year-old graduate of Karachi University: "My writing, like my thinking, is no Chinese puzzle of Kantian terminology, no Hegelian obfuscation, no Spinozist geometry; everything is clarity and order." In case we still were not convinced, he added: "Several times in near past my editor told me: 'Your writing is suggestive and interesting even when least convincing.'"

While living in Hong Kong, I also made a collection of surprising first names. People in Hong Kong were given Chinese names by their parents when they were born. Later on, in school, most children then chose an English first name to use with English-speaking people. Like children everywhere, many were blissfully free of conventional thinking. Some of the people I came across: Salad Lam, Boogie Chan, Dumbo Wan, Romeo Napoleon Wong, Dracula Wong, Lego Ho, Bacon Lee, and Nausea Yip.

SOME THINGS ARE not very important but should be included simply because they are peculiar.

One of the oddest assignments I had at the *Wall Street Journal* was to research a story on penis-enlargement pills.

It was 2003, and people frequently received junk email. Good filters weren't yet available. One of the most common nuisance email pitches was for penis-enlargement pills. It was an obvious scam, but one of the editors decided we should investigate these pills and find out exactly what they contained.

> Some things are not very important but should be included simply because they are peculiar.

And so it was that one day at work my supervisor, who happened to be a woman, instructed me to use my corporate credit card to order a bottle of penis-enlargement pills. (I can't remember how I recorded this purchase on my expense-claim form.) My assignment was to obtain the pills, find a chemistry lab to analyze them, and report on the contents. A colleague, Julia Angwin, traveled to Nanaimo, British Columbia, to visit a company promoting and selling the pills.

Finding the right sort of chemistry lab and negotiating a deal to analyze these pills kept me occupied for days.

Flora Research of San Juan Capistrano, California, conducted the tests for us and found significant levels of E. coli, yeast, mold, lead, and pesticide residues. "I think it's safe to say it has heavy fecal contamination," Michael Donnenberg, head of the infectious-diseases department at the University of Maryland, told us. That contamination might lead to diarrhea, among other things. As another expert told us, "You'd probably be spending more time in the bathroom than the bedroom with this product." In any case, I did not find it necessary to try the pills.

# CHAPTER 25

# *Inspiring Memoirs*

Reading other people's memoirs can stir up ideas that will help you enliven and enrich your own narrative. The list below is a tiny sample of the thousands of memoirs worth reading. By offering this list, I do not mean to suggest that a life story is worth telling only if it has literary merit or might be a bestseller. Rather, I hope you will find inspiration to tell your own story in your own way.

*The Autobiography of Benjamin Franklin,* completed around 1790, available for free at almost any library or on the internet. Franklin noted his "pleasure in obtaining any little anecdotes of my ancestors" and concluded rightly that his friends and family might one day have interest in the many things they didn't know about his life.

*Personal History* by Katharine Graham, 1997. "My parents' paths first crossed in a museum on 23rd Street in New York. It was Lincoln's Birthday, 1908." From the first two sentences, we know we are in good hands. The daughter of a Wall Street plutocrat, she grows up in mansions decked with Cézannes and Renoirs. On a girlhood visit to Europe, she meets Albert Einstein. ("His hair is positively a nest," she reports in a letter home.) In her memoir, she confesses her parents' character flaws and her own. She recounts the horrors of her life, notably her husband's suicide, as well as her insecurities and eventual triumphs as publisher of the *Washington Post*.

*Miss Aluminum* by Susanna Moore, 2020. The novelist describes her unlikely journey from neglected child to impoverished young adult to model, Hollywood muse, and literary success story.

*Liner Notes* by Loudon Wainwright III, 2017. The underappreciated singer-songwriter reveals that he needed only 12 minutes to write his only hit song, "Dead Skunk in the Middle of the Road," inspired by his own experience while driving in northern Westchester County, New York. In an uninhibited account that will offend some and amuse others, Wainwright chronicles his chronic philandering and his struggles with mild depression and a frail ego. His salvation was the charge he got from standing on stages and making people laugh.

*Boy* by Roald Dahl, 1984. In writing this slim and irresistible book, the author of children's stories left out what he called the boring details of his early life and concentrated on his odder experiences, such as when at eight years old he was caned for dropping a dead mouse into a jar of candy.

*Going Solo* by Roald Dahl, 1986. This book picks up where *Boy* ended, with Dahl being sent by the Shell Oil Company to work in East Africa. He sails to Dar es Salaam in Tanganyika with visions of jungle beasts dancing in his head. Though he is a civilian who works for an oil company, he finds himself at age 23 put in charge of herding all the German residents of Tanganyika into a prison camp at the outbreak of World War II. He admires elephants as he drives from Dar es Salaam to Nairobi to enlist in the Royal Air Force: "Their skin hung loose over their bodies like suits they had inherited from larger ancestors." Of the 16 young men in his pilot-training course, he was one of only three who survived the war. Still, "how many young men, I kept asking myself, were lucky enough to be allowed to go whizzing and soaring through the sky above a country as beautiful as Kenya?"

*A Cab at the Door* and *Midnight Oil* by V.S. Pritchett, 1968 and 1971. The master short-story writer tells his own story of growing up in a family that moved frequently around England, pursued by his father's creditors. Prodded into the leather trade as a clerk at age 15, he escaped five years later by moving to Paris, working in a photographic-supplies shop, and later establishing himself as a newspaper correspondent. Fleeing to France, he writes, was "a remedy for what I foolishly thought was my fatal disadvantage: lack of education." From his early days of reading French literature and gaping at Parisian sights, "I could not see that I had anything to say except that I was alive. I simply wanted to write two or three sentences, even as banal as the advertisement on a sauce bottle, and see them in print with my name beneath them." His first published work was a joke sent to the Paris edition of the *New York Herald*. Though he was paid nothing, he learned a lesson: "If one had nothing to say one could at any rate write what other people said." Later came the discovery that launched his career: "I was full of stories without knowing it." His disorderly childhood and eccentric family had already filled him with material for his best stories. You may be in the same position.

*The Years With Ross* by James Thurber, 1962. This book purports to be a biography of Harold Ross, the founding editor of the *New Yorker*, but is more of a memoir by Thurber of his amusing and baffling experiences with his former boss. Shunning chronology and any other conventional form of organization, Thurber apparently proceeded almost randomly from one memory to another, though he tried to organize them by themes. Somehow it works. For those who don't want to be shackled by chronology, Thurber produced a model of chaotic brilliance.

*Beeswing* by Richard Thompson, 2021. In a sometimes hilarious and often touching memoir, the British singer-songwriter recounts his early adventures. He is "always trying to figure out why I am the way I am," and that is what makes his tale so compelling.

*Conundrum* by Jan Morris, 1974. "I was three or four years old when I realized that I had been born into the wrong body, and should really be a girl," writes the Anglo-Welsh author formerly known as James Humphry Morris. As a boy, he felt himself an impostor. It was a matter of spirit more than sexuality: "That my conundrum might simply be a matter of penis or vagina, testicle or womb, seems to me still a contradiction in terms, for it concerned not my apparatus, but my *self*." He served happily as an intelligence officer in the British Army, even as Army life "confirmed my intuition that I was fundamentally different from my male contemporaries." He married a woman and had children but by midlife felt the unbearable strain of playing an unsuitable part. Hormone pills and surgery in Casablanca made him a woman. "The barrier between the genders," he wrote, "is flimsier now."

*Personal Memoirs of U.S. Grant* by Ulysses S. Grant, 1885. The former president resisted friends' suggestions that he should write his own story. Then, late in life, after a disastrous investment ruined him, he began writing as a way to dig himself out of debt. He recalled being repelled by his father's leather-tanning business in Ohio and devoting his youthful energies to farming and horse riding. When a fierce dog frightened one of his horses, Grant calmed the beast by blindfolding it with a bandana. Fear of failure made him wary of West Point. When his father arranged for his appointment to the military school, he yielded, though, as he put it, "I had not the faintest idea of staying in the Army even if I should be graduated, which I did not expect." Completed as he was dying of throat cancer, the memoir proved a commercial and critical success.

*I Came as a Shadow* by John Thompson, 2020. The late Georgetown University basketball coach recalls a childhood in which money was scarce but affection wasn't. His mother, who had a college degree, cleaned houses. His father, who was illiterate, worked at a tile factory. As a sixth grader, he was more than six feet tall and struggling academically. A teacher did her best to shield him from ridicule; he never forgot her kindness. As a recruiter, he didn't assume that a player's low grades or test scores reflected stupidity. In many cases, he knew, young Black men can be hobbled by low expectations.

*Off to the Side* by Jim Harrison, 2002. Of school, the author and poet says, "we failed each other." And so, as a teenager, he fled rural Michigan to explore the seamier corners of New York, Boston, and San Francisco. At other times he retreated into the natural world to recuperate from his depressions. He was "quite drunk with language" and declared himself a poet long before he learned to be one. His

184 — JAMES R. HAGERTY

memoir is rewarding both for the pleasure of Harrison's earthy company and for what he can teach us about telling a life story. His narrative is mixed with meditations on what life is all about and how and why to live it. He recounts his youth in more or less chronological order and then organizes the rest of the book by themes, including alcohol, hunting, religion, and the art of striptease.

*The Road from Coorain* by Jill Ker Conway, 1989. The first female president of Smith College tells the story of growing up in the 1930s and 1940s on a sheep farm in the Australian state of New South Wales, where "at sunset, rosella parrots, a glorious rosy pink, will settle on trees and appear to turn them scarlet." Her home lacked electricity and indoor plumbing. She learned to herd sheep and watched her father skin them. He drowned when she was 10; a brother died in a car accident. As a teenager, she considered herself an "ugly duckling" whose obsessions with Tudor history and Elizabethan drama made her a misfit.

*An American Childhood* by Annie Dillard, 1987. Born in 1945, the author recalls growing up in Pittsburgh at a time when the men rushed off to work each morning, while women stayed home. In astonishing detail, she evokes the boredom and wonders of being five years old on an endless summer day: "My project was to ride my swing all around, over the top. I bounced a ball against the house; I fired gravel bits from an illegal slingshot Mother gave me." It's hard to remember exactly how it felt to be a kid. Somehow Dillard remembers, and she reminds us in gloriously vivid prose.

*Chronicles: Volume One* by Bob Dylan, 2004. Dylan's memoir is an illustration of how to write a highly selective life story. The great mystifier was never going to give us a full and frank autobiography. This partial account nevertheless provides fascinating insights into certain aspects of his career. If you wish to reveal part of yourself in an entertaining fashion while preserving most of your secrets, this is a fine template.

# CHAPTER 26

# *What We Can Learn From Pepys*

It is safe to assume that Samuel Pepys (1633–1703) would be entirely forgotten today, except perhaps among the most diligent scholars of British naval history, if he had not written a diary between January 1660 and May 1669.

Pepys, a tailor's son who rose to become an administrator in the British Navy, doggedly kept an account of his day-to-day life, written in shorthand, recording both his triumphs and his vices, and fervently hoped that some of the secrets confessed in his diary would never be known to his contemporaries. Yet he also must have understood the importance of the record he kept: He made provisions in his will for the preservation of his library, including his six-volume diary, at "one of our Universities."

Whatever his motives, he left a lesson for us in the value and technique of preserving details of events great and small.

Yes, he described historic events, including the Restoration of the Stuart monarchy, the Great Fire of London, and a plague. But he was at least equally curious about himself and saw "his own mental and physical nature as not merely a legitimate but a valuable and glorious subject for exploration," as Claire Tomalin wrote in her 2002 biography of Pepys.

He wrote his life story in the form of a diary rather than by recollecting events years or decades later. The result is an unusual richness of detail.

What I treasure most are the vignettes of 17th-century life.

A "very fine dinner" includes "a dish of marrow bones; a leg of mutton; a loin of veal; a dish of fowl, three pullets, and two dozen of larks all in a dish; a great tart, a neat's tongue, a dish of anchovies; a dish of prawns and cheese."

He and his wife quarrel after he gets fed up with their dog "fouling the house" and banishes the beast to the cellar. They go to bed still angry; he dreams his wife has died, "which made me that I slept ill all night."

He resolves to avoid "strong drink" after finding "it makes me sweat and puts me quite out of order."

He recalls having endured a sermon at church and "spent (God forgive me) most of my time in looking upon Mrs. Butler." (One reason people still read Pepys is that he did not pretend to be any more virtuous than he was.)

In October 1660, he ventures to Charing Cross in London to see Maj. Gen. Thomas Harrison, who had been found guilty of regicide for his role in the execution of King Charles I. Harrison was "hanged, drawn, and quartered" and looked "as cheerful as any man could do in that condition."

Angry with his wife for leaving "her things lying about" in their home, he kicks "the little fine basket which I bought her in Holland and broke it, which troubled me after I had done it."

He notes lessons learned: "Thanks be to God, since my leaving drinking of wine, I do find myself much better and do mind my business better, and do spend less money, and less time lost in idle company."

Fed up with domestic squabbles, he tries remaining silent when his wife is in "an ill humour," rather than provoking her, and discovers this tactic has a calming effect.

He frets about how to discipline servants. At one point, Pepys resolves to punish "my man Will" for offenses including thievery, skipping church, and general insolence. "I reckoned all his faults, and whipped him soundly, but the rods were so small that I fear they did not much hurt to him, but only to my arm." At another point, after seeing Will walking "with his cloak flung over his shoulder, like a Ruffian," he gives the young man "two boxes on the ears, which I never did before, and so was after a little troubled at it."

He provides grooming tips: "So home, and had Sarah to comb my head clean, which I found so foul with powdering and other troubles, that I am resolved to try how I can keep my head dry without powder."

He laments the poor manners of his countrymen in mocking foreigners. Attendants of a Russian ambassador, arriving in London, wear fur caps and bring hawks as presents to the King. Pepys finds the foreigners handsome. "But Lord!" he writes, "to see the absurd nature of Englishmen, that cannot forbear laughing and jeering at everything that looks strange."

Attuned to fashion, he orders a velvet cloak and other fineries. In November 1663, after observing that the King's hair had gone "mighty gray," Pepys impulsively has his own locks cut and begins wearing a wig. He then discovers that other people do not necessarily pay close attention to his grooming. On the first Sunday after he began wearing the wig, "I thought that all the church would presently have cast their eyes all upon me, but I found no such thing."

He frequently attends plays. Two that didn't impress him were *Romeo and Juliet* and *A Midsummer Night's Dream*, the latter described as "the most insipid, ridiculous play that I ever saw in my life."

He is open to other forms of entertainment. In January 1664, he goes to Leadenhall Street to see a hanging and pays a shilling to stand on the wheel of a cart to get a better view. He has to wait more than an hour while the condemned man, one Turner, offers "discourses and prayers one after another, in hopes of a reprieve; but none came, and at last he was flung off the ladder in his cloake. A comely-looked man he was, and kept his countenance to the end."

He is furious when his wife buys a pair of earrings without his advance approval. She responds with "very foule words." He threatens to smash the jewelry. They go to bed angry.

188 — JAMES R. HAGERTY

Less than two months later, he buys her a pair of gloves trimmed with yellow ribbon to match a new petticoat. "She is so pretty that, God forgive me! I could not think it too much—which is a strange slavery that I stand in to beauty, that I value nothing near it."

Just as he recounts his many love affairs and dalliances, he records the joy he found in a new watch: "I cannot forbear carrying my watch in my hand in the coach all this afternoon, and seeing what o'clock it is one hundred times."

In July 1665, the plague is killing Londoners at an alarming rate, and Pepys vows to update his will in case he succumbs. Yet he cannot resist attending a wedding—and kissing the bride. He is proud of his "new coloured silk suit, and coat trimmed with gold buttons and gold broad lace round my hands, very rich and fine."

He frequently calculates his growing net worth, much of it in gold coins—"for which the great God of Heaven and Earth be praised!"

Fearing a Dutch invasion in 1667, he wears a girdle stuffed with gold so that "I may not be without something in case I should be surprised." He arranges for some of his gold to be buried near a country home and later has the irksome chore of digging it up and cleaning off the mud.

He admits an inability to resist women and music. "The truth is, I do indulge myself."

He does not regret all of his indulgences. Too many successful men, he observes, wait to indulge themselves until "it is too late for them to enjoy it."

> Start early, write while memories are fresh and vivid, and don't leave out the peculiar details of 21st-century life.

Preparing for a speech to Parliament in March 1668, he repairs to the Dog tavern for half a pint of fortified wine and follows it up with a dram of brandy, "and with the warmth of this did find myself in better order as to courage, truly." The speech is very well received.

At the end of April 1668, he sums up his preoccupations: "Thus ends this month; my wife in the country, myself full of pleasure and expense.... The kingdom in an ill state through poverty; a fleete going out, and no money to maintain it, or set it out; seamen yet unpaid, and mutinous when pressed to go out again. So we are all poor, and in pieces—God help us!"

The message for today's writers of life stories: Start early, write while memories are fresh and vivid, and don't leave out the peculiar details of 21st century life.

# CHAPTER 27

# My First Obituary

W HEN I WAS 21, IN the mid-1970s, decades before I ever imagined I might want to write obituaries for a living, I wrote my first. It was about Fred Eng.

During my freshman year at the University of North Dakota, Fred lived in the dorm room adjoining mine.

Fred came from Jamestown, North Dakota, where he was famous at his high school for having been arrested and fined $75 for indecent exposure after running naked—"streaking," we called it then— through a shopping mall in Fargo. By the time I met him in college, Fred had no clear sense of direction. Nor was he troubled by any excessive ambition.

Even getting out of bed was a challenge for Fred. At one point, he asked me to help rouse him in time for classes. Fred, a man of whims, drew up an elaborate contract authorizing me to enter his room at a certain hour each morning and douse him with a pitcher of ice water. He arranged for our solemn contract to be signed before a notary public.

Cold water in the face certainly did work better than any other alarm he had tried. It was a bonus that I happened to enjoy soaking his sleepy head. I was sorry my mission lasted only one day. After that, Fred made sure to lock his door.

He reverted to his routine. After the minimal exertions required to skip two or three lectures, he'd settle his long, lean body into a rocking chair, eat granola, and sip prune juice.

One surprising thing about Fred was that, despite his distaste for most types of effort, he was willing to write letters. We corresponded during summer vacations. In one of those letters, Fred outlined his approach to living: "For 10 long years, people told me to go, go, go, and me, I said no, no, no, slow, slow, slow."

The last time I saw Fred was in 1977, during a brief visit to his hometown of Jamestown. We met at a bar to play Fred's favorite sport, one that required very little exertion—pool. After several leisurely games of eight ball, I started to feel restless and announced that it was time for me to head home. Though Fred wanted to keep playing, I dashed off.

That summer he worked on a crew building log cabins in Montana. He sent me a startling update through the U.S. mail: "For the first time ever I've had a job I enjoy."

When I got back to the university that autumn, a friend gave me news I found hard to believe: A log had rolled off the roof of a cabin Fred's crew was erecting. The log hit Fred's head and killed him. He was 21.

I WROTE ABOUT Fred's life in a student newspaper. I'll give myself a C+ for my debut as an obituary writer. Though I quoted from his letters and managed to give some idea of Fred's sense of humor and quirks, I could have preserved much more of his story if I had interviewed Fred's family and other friends.

**Every life story has lessons, large or small.**

Every life story has lessons, large or small. In the case of Fred, one lesson applies to me: I should have stuck around that day in Jamestown for a few more games of pool with my friend.

CHAPTER 28

# A Ridiculously Short History of Obituaries

Before the invention of the printing press, obituaries appeared in other forms, including as epitaphs, such as this one from Egypt in the third century AD: "In peace and blessing Ama Helene, a Jew, who loves the orphans, [died]. For about 60 years her path was one of mercy and blessing; on it she prospered."

Plutarch, writing his brief biographies of prominent Greeks and Romans, was essentially compiling belated obituaries by sorting through legends and historical records. For instance, he did not attempt to describe every battle fought by Alexander the Great, but praised the Macedonian king for restraint and consideration in his treatment of the captured wife of the Persian King Darius III.

Early newspaper obituaries tended to be very brief, yet sometimes captured a picturesque detail. On May 14, 1795, the *Derby Mercury* in England reported the death of Christian Marshall of Overton, who lived to the age of 101 and "never took a dose of physic in her life—never wore a ribbon on her head—nor a buckle on her shoe."

From Pennsylvania's *Lancaster Intelligencer* of Dec. 3, 1800: "Died in this Borough Mr. Johann Geo. Doth, aged 74 years. He weighed upwards of 400 lbs."

YOURS TRULY — 193

The death in 1868 of James Buchanan, the 15th president of the United States and often considered among the worst, inspired this comment from New York's *Albany Evening Journal*: "No widow will mourn for him; no maimed soldier will drop a tear to his memory; no affranchised slave will think of him as a saviour; no grateful hosts of his countrymen will unite in a tribute of unfading affection. Selfish in his life, in his death he was left to himself."

Where was Buchanan's version of his own story? He told part of it in a book published two years before his death. It had an unpromising title: *Mr. Buchanan's Administration on the Eve of the Rebellion*. After a turgid account of the political and legislative battles leading up to the Civil War, Buchanan concluded, "I shall carry to my grave the consciousness that I at least meant well for my country."

The former president "blamed everybody but himself for the dissolution of the Union," Ted Sorensen wrote in 2010.

By fixating on an unwinnable argument over the causes of the war, Buchanan blew an opportunity to write what could have been a more interesting book, including candid reflections on his successes, his shortcomings, the rest of his life, and the forces that shaped him. We needed to meet the human, not just the resentful politician.

Long ago, newspapers recognized the difficulty of writing an adequate obituary when the best source, the deceased, was no longer available for comment. A headline from the *Seattle Post-Intelligencer* in 1890: "Obituaries All Ready: Many Men Have Written Their Own and Wisely."

In 1910, the *New Era* of Lancaster, Pennsylvania, grouped several obituaries under the headline: "Aged People Pass Away." In case readers had not noticed.

In the 1980s, the leading British newspapers, particularly the *Daily Telegraph* and the *Times*, discovered that obituaries could be a form of gossipy entertainment, just as tempting as the crime and sporting news. In 1991, the *Telegraph* published an obituary with this irresistible intro: "The Third Lord Moynihan, who has died in Manila, aged 55, provided through his character and career ample ammunition for critics of the hereditary principle. His chief occupations were bongo drummer, confidence trickster, brothel-keeper, drug-smuggler and police informer."

The rollicking British style of obituary writing influenced American obituary writers, though most of them, unlike their wilder London counterparts, were still restrained by the need to credit their sources and verify facts. Obituaries in the best American papers have become lively mini-biographies of all kinds of people—famous or obscure, male or female—rather than dull lists of achievements, honors, and tributes from cronies.

Obituary writing is now even sometimes seen as an art form. A collection of send-offs by one master—*52 McGs.: The Best Obituaries from Legendary* New York Times *Reporter Robert McG. Thomas Jr.*—was published in 2001.

In our era, obituaries have grown more interesting and amusing but not always more illuminating about the accidents, forces, and passions that shaped people's lives. We can do better.

CHAPTER 29

# A Little Is Way Better Than Nothing

Pete Correll (1941–2021) had an inspiring life story to tell but never found time to put it down on paper or tape.

His full name was Alston Dayton Correll Jr. An only child, he was known as Little Pete. His dad was Big Pete. Big Pete was a manager at J.C. Penney and later opened his own menswear store in Brunswick, a coastal town in Georgia.

Big Pete, who had a drinking problem, died when Little Pete was 12. The boy and his mother, Elizabeth, were left to run the store. They discovered that much of what they had thought was inventory consisted of empty boxes on the shelves. Other boxes, they found, contained empty liquor bottles. Somehow the widow and Little Pete sorted things out and found a way to run the business profitably.

No longer Little Pete, Correll started college at Georgia Tech. He dropped out and worked briefly at the New York Stock Exchange as a runner, delivering order slips to traders. Then he enrolled at the University of Georgia, where he majored in business. He also met Ada Lee Fulford, who was working on an education degree. They married in 1963.

196 — JAMES R. HAGERTY

Correll envisioned a career in retailing. He worked as a manager in a J.C. Penney store. Some of his friends urged him to think about a different career. Sensing better opportunities, he joined a pulp and paper mill as a supervisor. He later enrolled at the University of Maine and earned a master's degree in pulp and paper technology.

He supervised mills for Weyerhaeuser Co. and Mead Corp. and climbed into the executive ranks. In 1988, Georgia-Pacific Corp. appointed him as senior vice president for pulp and printing paper. He leapfrogged veteran Georgia-Pacific executives to become chief executive officer five years later. A local magazine ran a photo of him astride a Harley-Davidson motorcycle.

Georgia-Pacific, based in Atlanta, made pulp, paper, plywood, and gypsum wallboard. Sales of the building products lurched from boom to bust with the ups and downs of construction. Those swings made investors antsy and held down the value of the company's shares.

"One year you're the most admired management team in North America," Correll told the *Chicago Sun-Times* in 2001. "The next year you're the most hated, and you didn't do anything, except the price of plywood dropped in half."

He wanted steadier, recession-proof businesses. So, in 2000, the company purchased the maker of Quilted Northern toilet paper and Brawny paper towels.

Correll cheerfully embraced his role as "the king of toilet paper." He made it into a reliable laugh line: "Toilet paper is a wonderful product," he would deadpan. "Ninety-eight percent of the American public uses it." If you asked him what the other two percent were using, he would say he had no idea. "We don't have any research on that," he told the *New York Times*.

One occasional frustration was that the general public had no idea what Georgia-Pacific was. A hotel clerk, upon learning that Correll headed Georgia-Pacific, congratulated him for running "a damn good railroad."

Bargain hunters saw the company's value. Koch Industries Inc. agreed to pay $13.2 billion to buy Georgia-Pacific in 2005. Correll retired as chairman the next year.

Little Pete was now Rich Pete and, at 65 years old, could have devoted himself exclusively to playing golf and perhaps presiding over the occasional fundraising gala. He chose a more demanding task.

Atlanta's Grady Memorial Hospital, serving the metropolitan area's poor and uninsured, was a financial wreck. Correll, already known as someone willing and able to take on thankless civic chores, paid a visit to Grady. He saw patients on gurneys languishing in dingy halls. The charts were written by hand and duplicated with carbon paper. "It was like stepping back 30 years," he said.

Correll discussed the public hospital's crisis with a friend, Tom Bell, over a drink. They agreed that *someone* would have to rescue the hospital. "After a few more drinks," Correll told the *Atlanta Journal-Constitution*, "we decided it would be us."

They came up with a reorganization of the hospital's governance in 2008. One goal was to shift management of the hospital from political appointees to a new nonprofit corporation with directors who, it was hoped, would be more insulated from political pressures. Correll had to work hard to reassure civic leaders that the reorganization would not deprive poor people of services.

He also leaned on other Atlanta-area hospitals to support Grady. The richer suburban hospitals, Correll said, in his typical blunt fashion, would be in "deep doggie poop" if forced to take care of Grady's uninsured patients. Correll helped raise $300 million to upgrade Grady's antiquated equipment and facilities. He served as chairman of Grady for eight years.

Correll and his family talked about how to preserve his story and the lessons he had learned. Before they could make any progress, he was diagnosed with cancer. One of his friends had told his life story to a ghost writer. "Dad realized he was kind of out of time to do that," said his daughter, Elizabeth Correll Richards.

Eventually, he was so sick that his voice was slurred and most people couldn't understand what he was saying, but Elizabeth still could make out most of his words. She started looking over transcripts from interviews he had given over the years. When she found a gap in the story, she asked him to fill it in. He seemed eager to talk about his life.

Elizabeth asked questions such as, How did you choose a frater-
nity when you were in college? "An hour later," she told me, "he had
told a whole story about his college career." She took notes.

When Correll realized he was near death, in March 2021, he told
Elizabeth, "I really want to say something at my funeral."

She joked about bringing him to his funeral as a hologram. They
decided someone else, the preacher, could read his words to the con-
gregation. He wanted no eulogies at the funeral, no boring recitation
of his many awards and achievements, already familiar to his friends
and family. There would be only his own message about the way he
wanted to be remembered.

Correll's message was brief, but "it took a couple of months to get
it right," Elizabeth said. He talked. She recorded with her iPhone.

Some 800 people attended the funeral at the First Presbyterian
Church of Atlanta on June 2, 2021. Rev. Tony Sundermeier read Correll's words:

Thank you for coming. Since Tony is reading this note,
I must be dead.

But there are a few things I want to say to you.
Please don't be sad, I have led a rich full life driven by
three things.

First, I am a predestined Presbyterian. All my life I
have known that God put me on this earth to do something, I just never really knew what that was. Clearly
Grady was it. How else can you explain a poor southern
boy, raised by a single parent in Brunswick, Georgia,
never having been to Atlanta, Georgia, being the cata-
lyst to drive Grady. God must have been preparing me
for this my whole life. Think about it—this poor boy led
a group of Atlanta businessmen to save Grady hospital.
How unthinkable is that, especially without a plan.
When people say to me, God does not have a plan for
everyone's life, I want to laugh in their face. When God
led me all over the U.S.A., he was preparing me for one

task—saving Grady. That was 70 years after I was born. That, ladies and gentlemen, is the definition of long-term planning and what God has in store for you in your life, if you chose to follow His direction.

The second thing in my life was a strong mother. My father died when I was 12 years old. He was a nice man, but he was an abusive alcoholic. We were bankrupt and were too dumb to know it, so Mother and I set about paying all of our bills and running a men's store in Brunswick, Georgia. That experience taught me well the value of cash, which business students never understand. They can read a balance sheet and income statement but can't read a cash flow statement. There is nothing more sobering than looking in the cash drawer at the end of the day and seeing if there was more or less money in it than when the day began. That premise taught at Correll's Men Shop drove my whole business career. Nothing matters but cash.

The third driving force in my life, another strong woman, Ada Lee. A sweet young girl from Swainsboro, Georgia, who believed that everything would always be all right in life, a true Pollyanna. I moved her all over the country from Georgia to Virginia to Maine to North Carolina to Arkansas to Seattle to Dayton, Ohio, and finally back to Atlanta. All the time she kept saying this is what God had planned for you, say yes. It got so I would come home from work and say, honey we are moving. Not even asking where, she would start packing. The Corrells—two small children and a dog—would take off. When you ask Alston and Elizabeth where they are from, they are stumped. They have been exposed to so many places and situations. My home has become where the four are, not a given place with a given name.

Tony will be at the back door accepting memberships to the Presbyterian Church. May God be with you

all and may you always know I led the perfect life, and
it is time for me to leave the field of play.
    God bless you all.

Then a brass band played Correll's choice for the finale, "When
the Saints Go Marching In." Starting slow and mournful, the band finished with brio.

WEEKS LATER, ELIZABETH was still just getting started on organizing
all the interview transcripts. But at least she knew exactly what her
father saw as his mission in life.

"It's actually pushed us in our family into saying we've really got
to document things better," Elizabeth told me. "Even if you don't
think you're important, you're important to somebody."

    Amen.

CHAPTER 30

# *Summing Up*

Y OU MAY BE LIKE VARTAN GREGORIAN, Peter Kann, or Mort Crim and write an entire book. You could turn your story into a parable and devotional like the Lindner brothers. You may leave a recording like Bob Greene's dad—or some dictated notes like Pete Correll.

If you start early enough, thoughts about where you are heading in life may improve your sense of direction and purpose.

Save scraps and artifacts—letters, diaries, programs, concert tickets, social media postings, annotated photographs. Put them on a USB memory stick and on paper in a sturdy box for safekeeping. Learn from Pepys, Roald Dahl, Ben Franklin, and others who accounted for themselves in amusing and instructive ways.

Don't let anyone tell you that sharing your story is selfish, a sign of conceit or vanity. It's an act of generosity. It's a chance to tell the rest of us what you were up to, why parts of it worked out better than others, and what you learned. It's a way to acknowledge your failures, explain a few things your friends and family could never understand, celebrate whatever good fortune you've had, and thank those who gave you a hand or a smile when you needed it. You can make people cry and make them laugh. They will need to do both when you're gone.

Tell your story!

It isn't going to be perfect. It may be clumsy and disjointed. You probably will end up leaving out or glossing over some important things because they are too embarrassing, incriminating, or likely to hurt someone. You might misspell a few words, violate a grammatical rule or two, and forget to mention an in-law. You may never finish the project.

**Tell your story!**

That's okay. An imperfect, incomplete story, offering whatever you can muster to explain yourself and share the lessons you've learned is a precious gift to your friends, loved ones, and maybe even posterity in general.

As for the memories you will resurrect and the insights into living you may discover, those are gifts to yourself.

# Acknowledgments

Thanks to all the people who have helped me tell the life stories of hundreds of fascinating people, to my *Wall Street Journal* colleagues who have instructed and inspired me, to Jay Hershey for suggesting the article that grew into this book, to Bob Greene for sharing his experience with recording life stories, to Peter Johnson for reading a rough draft and making good suggestions, to Robert Dilenschneider for making an introduction that led to the publication of this book, to Michaela Hamilton for seeing value in the idea for this book and encouraging me to write it, to my parents for teaching me the fundamentals of writing and reporting, to my sister Gail for inspiring me to become a journalist, to my children for listening to some of my stories more than once, and to my wife, Lorraine, for her unwavering kindness and support.

# About the Author

JAMES R. HAGERTY, known as Bob, has worked as a staff reporter and editor at the *Wall Street Journal* and the *International Herald Tribune* for more than 40 years. A graduate of the University of North Dakota with a degree in economics, he was based in New York, Atlanta, London, Brussels, Paris, and Hong Kong before settling with his wife and two children in Pittsburgh, Pennsylvania. Since 2016, he has been the *Wall Street Journal's* full-time obituary writer. He also is a frequent writer of the entertaining stories known as A-Heds that appear daily on the front page of the *Wall Street Journal*. One of his most popular stories, "When Mom Goes Viral," was included with 20 other articles in *Dogfight at the Pentagon*, a collection of *Wall Street Journal* A-Heds. He is the author of *The Fateful History of Fannie Mae: New Deal Birth to Mortgage Crisis Fall*. Visit him on Facebook or Twitter @JamesRHagerty.